INSIGHT COMPACT GUIDE

SRI Lanka

MW00723992

Compact Guide: Sri Lanka is the ultimate quick-reference guide to this fascinating destination. It tells you everything you need to know about the island's attractions, from its serene Buddhist shrines and vibrant Hindu temples to its mountain peaks and tea plantations, plus its wonderful beaches and its lively capital, Colombo.

This is one of 130 Compact Guides, combining the interests and enthusiasms of two of the world's best-known information providers: Insight Guides, whose innovative titles have set the standard for visual travel guides since 1970, and Discovery Channel, the world's premier source of nonfiction television programming.

APA PUBLICATIONS
Part of the Langenscheidt Publishing Group

Insight Compact Guide: Sri Lanka

Written by: Martina Miethig
English version by: Paul Fletcher
Edited by: Maria Lord
Photography by: David Henley
Additional photography by: Panos Pictures
Cover picture by: Glen Allison/Stone
Design: Graham Mitchener
Picture Editor: Hilary Genin
Maps: Polyglott
Design Concept: Carlotta Junger

Editorial Director: Brian Bell
Managing Editor: Tony Halliday

NO part of this book may be reproduced, stored in a retrieval system or transmitted in any form or by any means (electronic, mechanical, photocopying, recording or otherwise), without prior written permission of *Apa Publications*. Brief text quotations with use of photographs are exempted for book review purposes only.

CONTACTING THE EDITORS: As every effort is made to provide accurate information in this publication, we would appreciate it if readers would call our attention to any errors and omissions by contacting:
Apa Publications, PO Box 7910, London SE1 1WE, England.
Fax: (44 20) 7403 0290
e-mail: insight@apaguide.demon.co.uk

Information has been obtained from sources believed to be reliable, but its accuracy and completeness, and the opinions based thereon, are not guaranteed.

© 2001 APA Publications GmbH & Co. Verlag KG Singapore Branch, Singapore.

First Edition 2001
Printed in Singapore by Insight Print Services (Pte) Ltd
Original edition © Polyglott-Verlag Dr Bolte KG, Munich

Worldwide distribution enquiries:
APA Publications GmbH & Co. Verlag KG (Singapore Branch)
38 Joo Koon Road, Singapore 628990
Tel: (65) 865-1600, Fax: (65) 861-6438

Distributed in the UK & Ireland by:
GeoCenter International Ltd
The Viables Centre, Harrow Way, Basingstoke,
Hampshire RG22 4BJ
Tel: (44 1256) 817987, Fax: (44 1256) 817-988

Distributed in the United States by:
Langenscheidt Publishers, Inc.
46–35 54th Road, Maspeth, NY 11378
Tel: (1 718) 784-0055, Fax: (1 718) 784-0640

www.insightguides.com

SRI Lanka

Introduction

Places

Culture

Travel Tips

◁ **Nuwara Eliya (p55)**
This hill station in the midst of Sri Lanka's tea growing region offers an escape from the heat of the coast.

▷ **Adam's Peak (p57)**
Sunrise viewed from the summit of this sacred mountain with fellow pilgrims is one of the greatest sights in Sri Lanka.

▽ **Anuradhapura (p43)**
Part of the 'Cultural Triangle' and one of the greatest monastic cities of antiquity, Anuradhapura is an important pilgrimage site.

△ **Polonnaruwa (p47)**
The medieval Sinhalese capital of the island was the site of an extraordinary artistic renaissance.

◁ **Unawatuna (p69)**
This beautiful, coral-fringed bay has golden sands and wonderfully clear water.

△ **Sigiriya (p50)**
Coupled with its exquisite murals, the spectacular situation of this site, perched on top of a massive rock, makes this one of the wonders of the island.

△ **Temple of the Tooth (p36)** This temple in the city of Kandy, home to a tooth of the Buddha, is one of the most sacred sites of the Buddhist world. The procession of the *perahera* here is not to be missed.

▽ **Colombo Pettah (p31)**
The capital's vibrant and crowded bazaar is a place for walking, shopping and gaining an insight into the lives of ordinary Sri Lankans.

△ **Yala (p73)**
Sri Lanka's top national park, famed for its population of wild elephants and leopards.

◁ **Sinharaja (p62)**
The last rainforest in Sri Lanka, now protected, has a great variety of indigenous flora and fauna.

Island of Serendipity

Sri Lanka has had a string of identities and has been known under a range of nicknames and pseudonyms. To Prince Vijaya and the founders it was *Tambapanni*, after the copper-coloured beach on which they landed. In the reign of the Roman Emperor Claudius, a sea captain working for Annius Plocamus, a tax collector, in the Red Sea, was caught in a monsoon that swept his boat off course and dumped him on the island 15 days later. For him *Tambapanni* was too much of a mouthful and became *Taprobane*. The geographer Ptolemy made a slight change, showing it on his 2nd-century AD map as *Taprobanam*.

Opposite: Tangalla coastline
Below: a Sinhalese guide
Bottom: monks near Hikkaduwa

Arab traders could have told Annius Placamus's captain that if he waited a while a different monsoon would blow him back to Arabia, or if he liked, East Africa. They relied on these winds to go back and forth, knew the island well and called it *Serendib*, a corruption of a Sanskrit word *Sinhaladvipa*. But the 18th-century English novelist, Horace Walpole, stuck to the Arabic for his fairy-tale, *The Three Princes of Serendib*, and used it to coin the word 'serendipity', meaning discovery by happy accident.

It was the Portuguese captain, Edward Barbosa, visiting in 1515, who arrived at the name *Celāo*, a corruption of the Chinese *Si-Lan*, which to Europeans became *Seylan*. The Dutch settled for *Zeilan*, the English compromise was Ceylon. But the Sinhalese, who had lived on the island for many hundreds of years, always preferred *Lanka*, and it officially changed to Sri Lanka in 1972 (the prefix means 'holy' or 'beautiful').

CONTRASTING CULTURES

Although few people arrive on Sri Lanka by happy accident nowadays – for many years Western tourists have been including this tropical paradise on their list of exotic holiday destinations – the increasing numbers who do come here are surprised to discover such cultural diversity, varied landscapes and palm-lined, picture-postcard

Below: traditional way of life
Bottom: a Tamil woman

beaches, historic and sacred remains, colourful pilgrimages, exotic wildlife and flora, and faded colonial charm.

Young people in Colombo prefer wearing jeans to the traditional sarong, cleaning a temple is now a job for the vacuum cleaner rather than a brush made from coconut fibres, and incense sticks are lit for the dilapidated oil pump rather than to create good *karma*. Even so, in some of the impoverished regions, traditional ways of life carry on.

However much the Buddha is revered and however generous the sacrificial offerings to the gods and saints may be, the menace of war has still not been assuaged. Visitors are often thoroughly bewildered by the conflict that rages between the Sinhalese Buddhists and the Tamil Hindus, followers of two largely peace-loving religions. By and large, the war is contained in the northern and eastern parts where most Tamils live.

The closure of some parts of the country to visitors creates an incentive to explore other areas more closely. If you walk or cycle down a side road, just a few minutes from a busy tourist centre, you will find stunning scenery and people as friendly, polite and easy-going as ever.

SITUATION AND SIZE

The tropical island of Sri Lanka lies at the southern tip of the Indian subcontinent, 650km (403 miles) north of the equator. A chain of islets, shallows, sandbanks and coral reefs, collectively known as Adam's Bridge, appears to cross the 35-km (22-mile) wide Palk Strait and to link the north of Sri Lanka with the south of India. The shape of the island has aroused the imagination of both the explorers who discovered it and its inhabitants. Is it a pearl, a jewel or a mango fruit? Given the fertility and beauty of Sri Lanka, any of the three could serve as a symbol. More prosaically, and somewhat insensitively for the island's Buddhists and Muslims, Dutch explorers thought of it as a Westphalian ham.

Covering an area of 65,000 sq.km (25,000 sq.miles), Sri Lanka is roughly as big as Belgium and Holland combined. Some 434km (267 miles) long and 225km (140 miles) across at its widest point, the island offers a wealth of remarkable sights.

Below: Duhinda Falls
Bottom: the tea fields

SCENIC DIVERSITY

The scenic diversity is unique. If there were competition for shades of green, then Sri Lanka would be the clear winner. These range from the bright green of the coconut and palmyra palm to the mist-shrouded green shades of the rainforest, from the vivid green to yellowy rice fields on the plains to the deep green tea bushes in the hill country, and from the mangrove thickets and bamboo forests by the coasts and river banks to the lush green rubber tree plantations. Green as far as the eye can see, as far as the turquoise ocean. The beaches are protected by coral reefs, sandbanks and lagoons, and many of the gently curving bays are perfect for bathing.

The vegetation varies from marshland by the south and west coast to dry savannah in the north and northeast, from small expanses of desert on the Jaffna peninsula to large areas of salt lakes and grassy plains in the southeast of the island. Rising out of the lowlands in the southern and

central regions are hill ranges and steep-sided rock fortresses, such as Sigiriya (2,000m/6,550ft), all dominated by Mount Pidurutalagala, at 2,524m (8,280ft) the highest summit in Sri Lanka, and Adam's Peak (2,243m/7,359ft), a sacred place of pilgrimage. With so many plateaux and gorges, valleys and basins, mountain peaks and tea-smothered hillsides, Sri Lanka's Central Highlands region must surely be one of the most delightful landscapes in Asia.

Adam's Peak

Some 25 rivers wind their way down to the coast from the upland region, many of them plunging down steep slopes as waterfalls. The longest and most important river in Sri Lanka is the Mahaweli Ganga.

CLIMATE AND WHEN TO GO

The tropical monsoon climate bestows an average temperature of 30°C (86°F) and a 90 percent humidity level on the island. By the coast a pleasant breeze blows throughout the year. In the hill country, mainly around Nuwara Eliya, temperatures can fall to 10°C (50°F), but water temperature remains at a constant 27°C (80°F).

Monsoon winds and mountains split the country into two climate zones: the damp southwest and the drier northeast. Southwesterly monsoons bring rain to the west coast, southwest coast and hinterland from May to September/October, while northeasterly monsoons keep the east coast and the northeastern lowlands wet between November and January/February. During the monsoon season, the seas become choppy and, with the exception of a few sheltered spots, bathing is not recommended.

The best time to visit the west and southwest is between October and March/April. Around Kandy the driest time is between January and April/May. However, rain should not be a deterrent. A tropical shower can be very heavy, but does not usually last long. An umbrella is never out of place in Sri Lanka. You may need it to keep the rain off, and you will need it to provide protection from the hot sun.

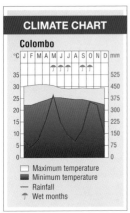

CLIMATE CHART

Colombo

°C	J F M A M J J A S O N D	mm
35		525
30		450
25		375
20		300
15		225
10		150
5		75
0		0

☐ Maximum temperature
■ Minimum temperature
— Rainfall
🌂 Wet months

FLORA

Over 3,000 species of flowers grow on the island. They mainly display their magnificent colour between March and May and include the 1,000 or so wild orchid species, the fiery red flamboyant trees and hibiscus bushes, long-stemmed lotus and white temple blossoms of the cannon ball (or *sal*) tree, wildly fragrant frangipani blooms and verdant rhododendron bushes. The most famous tree in Sri Lanka – the sacred Bo tree in Anuradhapura, *Ficus religiosa* – is also said to be the oldest. Many different types of palms and banana trees help to create the typically tropical landscape.

The tea and rubber plantations, built up over the past few centuries, have pushed back the jungle frontiers. The Sinharaja *(see page 62)* is the country's last great primeval rainforest; the Udawattekele Sanctuary *(see page 38)* in Kandy is slightly smaller. Beneath the dense canopy in both of these reserves, you can listen in on the buzzing and humming of a real rainforest, surrounded by giant trees overgrown with climbers and lianas – and also meet the leeches.

The Botanical Gardens in Peradeniya near Kandy *(see page 39)* and in Hakgala near Nuwara Eliya give visitors a colourful overview of the island's flora. The finest natural parks are Adam's Peak Wilderness *(see page 57)*, Horton Plains *(see page 56)* and the Knuckles Range.

Nature Reserves
Sri Lanka has 11 national parks and 70 nature reserves. With a little luck, patience and a good set of binoculars, you will be able to glimpse a sloth bear (melursus ursinus) or a leopard. The continued existence of the wild cats is under threat, but some remain in Wilpattu National Park, which is closed for the time being because of the civil war.

Below: flowering hibiscus
Bottom: collecting rubber

THE ANIMAL WORLD

Below: three playful monkeys
Bottom: collecting coral

Everything that walks or flies on the island can be observed at close quarters in Dehiwala Zoo near Colombo *(see page 34)*. Water buffalo, white zebus and several hundred elephants are still used as beasts of burden. Blue whales, sperm whales and dolphins can be seen off the coast in February and March, particularly near Trincomalee, Hambantota or off the Great Basses Reef *(see page 73)*. During the European winter some 440 bird species gather by the lakes and in the national parks.

But even in Colombo the chorus of exotic songbirds can be heard in the morning and at night. Peacocks, herons, deer, monkeys and crocodiles abound. You may even see a monitor lizard while out strolling along the beach in the evening. Geckos darting about in search of insects are ever-present on walls.

CORAL REEFS

The famous coral banks near Hikkaduwa are no longer what they were. For many years overloaded glass-bottom boats have being passing within a hair's breadth of the sensitive underwater treasures. The removal of the corals for the production of lime has reduced the effect of these natural breakwaters and the south coast road now faces the risk of flooding. In Negombo the beach

has had to be artificially restored. Thoughtless tourists who buy souvenirs made from coral are compounding the destruction of Sri Lanka's maritime world already caused by lime factories and fishermen using dynamite.

ELEPHANTS

Encounters with wild elephants are becoming rare events. Officially numbers are put at between 2,000 and 4,000, but in fact there are far fewer. In the Yala and Uda Walawe national parks visitors still have a good chance of seeing at least some of the hundred or so surviving grey giants, possibly even a whole herd.

The *Elephas maximus maximus*, to give the Ceylon elephant its correct name, is increasingly being driven out of its natural habitat and into the national parks. Because the elephants trample through villages and sugar cane plantations on their traditional route to watering holes and feeding grounds, there have been frequent deaths – on both sides.

Even in Sri Lanka, where the elephant has for thousands of years been treated as a revered friend and cultural icon, the pachyderms are not safe from ivory thieves. The Sri Lankan government is hoping to put a stop to these killings. Prison and a hefty fine await any poachers caught in the act. Animal protection societies – which have existed on the island for over100 years – are talking about creating 'jungle corridors' through inhabited regions to protect both people and animals. The elephant orphanage in Pinnawela *(see page 40)* is also helping with the preservation of these magnificent creatures.

TURTLES

Most superstitions harm nobody, but there are some practices that need to be discouraged. Many Sri Lankan men, for example, believe that the consumption of turtles' eggs can boost their sex drive. The fact that the animals have been protected species since 1972 worries them as little as it does the hundreds of souvenir shop owners

Snakes

Sri Lanka may have the world's highest death rate from snake bites, but tourists rarely come across these deadly reptiles. Of the 93 snake species found on the island, five are extremely poisonous, namely the cobra, two types of viper and two types of krait. Tall grass, dense undergrowth, rocks, jungle paths and fields are their preferred hideouts. As a safety measure, humans are advised to carry a stick, tread heavily, wear boots and thick socks and hold a torch in the dark. If a member of your party is bitten, immediately immobilise the limb in a horizontal position and apply a broad, firm bandage to the bitten area and, if possible, round the entire limb. Do not attempt to suck out the venom. Exertion and excitement should be avoided to prevent an increase in blood circulation.

Elephant at Peak Wilderness

A Matter of Survival

Sri Lanka could be a safe haven for turtles. Of the eight remaining turtle species, five lay their eggs on the Sri Lankan coast during the breeding season (December to February). Experts reckon that out of 1,000 eggs, only one sexually mature turtle will survive. These creatures are threatened not only by superstition, greed and predatory birds, but also by hotel construction as developers encroach on their nesting sites.

along the southwest coast who continue to sell tortoiseshell illegally. Nobody takes the protection order or the law seriously. Even government-run shops sell tortoiseshell products, some of which have been smuggled in from the Maldives.

To earn a few rupees, boys go out on to the beach at night to steal eggs from turtle nests, even while the mother is still laying them in the warm sand. Dealers pay two rupees per egg, so for 100 eggs the money makes a good sideline for the often impoverished families who live in the coastal villages. For many years now, animal protection organisations and hotels have been providing some competition. The Robinson Club Hotel in Bentota, for example, will pay the nest robbers four rupees per egg. These are then left to hatch in the hotel's secure 'hatchery'.

It takes about 50 days for the baby turtles to emerge from their eggs. They must stay in the seawater basin for no more than three days, otherwise they lose their natural instinct for survival in the ocean. The young turtles must also only be released at night or they will probably fall victim to predatory birds.

Most of the turtle breeding stations do not fulfil these conditions. They charge an admission fee to tourists and keep the babies, only taking them down to the sea several weeks, even months, later. For a small sum they will even introduce them to the sea in the heat of the day so that holiday-makers can photograph the episode. This means almost certain death for the young turtles. Visitors should refuse such photo opportunities.

Hawksbill turtle

THE TREE OF LIFE

The coconut palm in the soft light of evening – for Europeans this epitomises the romantic side of the Tropics. But behind this idyllic picture post-card image lies one of nature's miracles. For centuries, the inhabitants of these regions have understood the tree's gifts – from the roots to the end of the palm frond. It is impossible to imagine Sri Lankan cooking without coconut flesh, as it helps to tone down the extreme spiciness of a lot of curry dishes. The juice from a king coconut *(thambili)* is deliciously refreshing, the oil squeezed from the flesh is used for frying and processed into shampoos and soap, the fibres from the shell are twisted together to make string and rope, mats and brooms. The timber and the palm leaves find a use in house and boat construction.

Even the local firewater, *arrack*, is made from the coconut palm. This high-alcohol drink is made from fermented palm wine or toddy. Toddy tappers balance on ropes at dizzying heights to pass from one palm tree to the next.

Each year the flowers on one tree yield on average some 270 litres (60 gallons) of palm wine. The juice is then processed into a syrup and brown sugar known as *jaggery*. What is left of the tree is then used as firewood or fed to animals.

POPULATION

The 18.7 million inhabitants of Sri Lanka are mainly concentrated in the fertile southwest of the country, in Colombo and in the hill country. More than two-thirds of the islanders live and work outside the towns. Sri Lanka is still an agricultural country with many small settlements where homes are made from clay, ox-drawn ploughs turn over the soil and the work in the fields is carried out manually.

Below: East Coast woman and child
Bottom: fresh vegetable stall near Kandy

Everyday conditions for Sri Lankans are better than in many other developing countries. Free medicines, for example, have raised life expectancy to 70. This and a high birth rate have led to an above-average population growth. Thanks to the government's family planning programme, the birth rate has slowed (to about 1.2 percent per year).

Despite the relatively high educational standards (illiteracy rates are 8 percent for men, 15 percent for women), young people suffer from the high level of unemployment, currently 14 percent. Many high-school graduates and academics are without work. Skilled and unskilled workers often seek a way out of their plight by signing up to guest-worker contracts in the Middle East or by emigrating to one of the industrialised countries. If all else fails, young people have to turn to dubious ways of earning a living, such as prostitution *(see page 23)*.

Below: elderly man in Kalutara
Bottom: Kandy schoolchildren

ETHNIC COMPOSITION

The largest ethnic group in Sri Lanka are the Sinhalese (74 percent), predominantly followers of Buddhism. Their ancestors who emigrated to Sri Lanka from northern India in the 5th century BC were Indo-European peoples who had arrived in northern South Asia 1,000 years previously. The 3 million or so Tamils, mainly Hindus, make up

about 18 percent of the population. They can be subdivided into two groups: the ancestors of the Sri Lankan Tamils moved to the island from southern India in antiquity; the so-called Indian Tamils, who number about a million, mostly living in the 'hill country', were brought over by the English in the 1830s and later to work on the plantations. Almost all now have Sri Lankan nationality.

The original Sri Lankan Tamils live mainly in the north and east, where there was once a Tamil kingdom, Eelam, and where demands for an autonomous Tamil state *(Tamil Eelam)* originate.

LANGUAGE AND OTHER PEOPLES

Tamils and Sinhalese speak Tamil and Sinhala respectively, which have different origins and written forms. Tamil is of Dravidian (South Indian) origin, quite distinct from Sinhalese with its Indo-European roots. Disputes over language *(see page 18)* have played a large part in the centuries-old conflict between the two ethnic groups.

About 1 million Sri Lankans are Moors, the descendants of Arab seafarers who settled in Sri Lanka and who continue to dominate the jewellery trade. The Burghers have a lighter skin and more pronounced 'Western' features— their forefathers filled the ranks of the colonial masters. This group and the Malays each make up about 40,000.

ETHNIC CONFLICT

Even 2,000 years on there is still no sign of an end to the conflict between Tamils and Sinhalese. The dispute was intensified during the colonial era as the British changed the balance between the two ethnic groups by bringing Tamils across from southern India to work on the plantations and in administrative posts. But when independence was granted in 1948, any preferential treatment that the Tamils had enjoyed came to an end.

Now the Sinhalese had the upper hand. *Sinhala* replaced English as the state language and Buddhism became the state religion. The Tamils felt their cultural identity was under threat, and the

The Veddas

The Wanniyala-Aetto ('forest beings') are the indigenous people of Sri Lanka. Known as 'Veddas' in Sinhalese, these hunter-gatherers have lived in a sustainable relationship to their tropical forest environment for the past 18,000 years. Having survived 2,500 years of settlement of their island, first by Sinhalese and later by Tamil migrants from India, five centuries of Portuguese, Dutch and British colonisation, the Wanniyla-Aetto were evicted from what was left of their ancestral forests by the Sri Lankan Government to make way for the Maduru Oya National Park in 1983. Since then, the Veddas, who now number only about 2,500, have been battling for their very survival as a distinct ethnic group.

A Vedda man, one of the indigenous people of the island

👁 **View from the Street**
The people of this war-torn country can only hope that the hardliners on both sides eventually soften their stance. In the southwest and in Colombo at least, Sinhalese and Tamils, Hindus, Buddhists, Christians and Muslims live in a peaceful harmony. Every Sri Lankan you meet swears to having a Tamil or Sinhalese friend and longs for an end to the conflict. Just how deep the roots of hatred and racism penetrate on both sides is very hard for outsiders to assess.

Below: Tamil Tigress, Jaffna
Bottom: LTTE memorial

seeds were sown for a minority backlash. Since the 1970s the dispute has grown into one of the world's bloodiest guerrilla wars. Terrorism and persecution have relentlessly eroded hopes for negotiations and amnesties.

The discrimination felt by the Tamils can be understood from the dispute over language. It is true that Tamil is now the second state language, at least on paper, but Tamils still receive official letters in Sinhala, and at police stations or in post offices the Tamil language is only rarely understood. Arrests and raids against the Tamil population are commonplace.

CIVIL WAR

The conflict in Sri Lanka took a decided turn for the worse in 1983 when an attack by the LTTE (Liberation Tigers of Tamil Eelam) on the army in Jaffna killed one officer and 12 soldiers. Hardline Buddhist nationalists, including the clergy, used this as an excuse to embark on a pogrom against the Tamil population. Hundreds died throughout the country. Separatist guerrilla activity intensified and full-blown civil war ensued. Since 1983, there have been at least 50,000 lives lost on both sides. According to the UN, 12,000 people have 'disappeared'. Between 500,000 and 1 million Tamils from the Northern and Eastern Province have become homeless and live as 'displaced persons' either with relatives or in the 500 or so camps scattered around the country.

All ethnic groups have been affected by the civil war. The Tamil guerrillas targeted moderate Tamil as well as Sinhalese politicians in order to extinguish any internal competition.

In the late 1980s the JVP also engaged in acts of terrorism against the Sri Lankan population. This group, a militant 'Popular Liberation Front' made up of nationalist Sinhalese carried out bomb attacks in the south, demanding the withdrawal of the hated Indian 'peacekeepers'. But government soldiers and the Indian contingent were equally brutal. Amnesty International claim there has been indiscriminate killing, torture and civilian 'disappearances' for years, most of them victims of death squads and private armies. Recently mass graves of Tamil civilians have been uncovered in Jaffna, allegedly the result of government terror campaigns.

Sinhalese politicians declared themselves willing to seek compromise but have recently become much more hardline following the major defeat at Elephant Pass in 2000. The racial hatred seems to be abating, as does the support of the Tamil population for the terrorists. However, hopes for the peace process, which started in 1994, have receded following bomb attacks in Kandy and Colombo, continuing atrocities carried out by government troops and president Chandrika Kumaranatunga's vow to wipe the Tigers out militarily.

The rebels refuse to give up their arms before negotiations begin. President Kumaratunga had promised more autonomy for the Tamils in the northeast by creating a federal system, but she sent lower-ranking politicians to the negotiating table who lacked credibility. The LTTE demands a third of the country including economically strategic areas such as Trincomalee harbour, but the Tamils represent only a fifth of Sri Lanka's population and more than 50 percent live in the southwest and in the hill country.

As a result of these complexities, any meaningful agreement appears to be a long way off.

Below: returning refugees
Bottom: relatives of the disappeared

Religious Sensibilities
To avoid hurting the religious feelings of your hosts, follow a few simple rules. Take off your shoes and place them outside the door before entering a temple, temple ruins or house and remove your sunhat or cap. If you are visiting a temple, don't wear sleeveless blouses and shorts. It is unacceptable to smoke within sight of a Buddha figure.

Below: cutting jak fruit
Bottom: a chat on the beach

CONDUCT

Sri Lankans are open and curious towards visitors. Many speak English and it is easy to get into a conversation with the locals. It is worth noting the way in which a question is answered affirmatively. The head waggles slowly from side to side, a mixture of swinging and shaking, which you will almost certainly interpret the first time as a 'no'.

Many women still wear the traditional sari, a 6-m (20-ft) length of material wrapped skilfully and attractively around the body. Away from the towns, most men wear a sarong, a thigh-length loincloth. It is the tradition to eat with the right hand. The Sri Lankans believe that rice and curry simply taste better that way. Many Sri Lankans chew betel nuts and then spit out the red juice.

The beaches in Sri Lanka are not private property and many villagers and fishermen use the beach as a toilet. Matters of bodily hygiene are open to public gaze as only 25 percent of Sri Lankans have their own bath. Men and women can be seen – usually at separate times – standing by the water fountain, under waterfalls or in the river washing and cleaning their teeth. Although such a scene may make an interesting snap, keep your camera in its case to avoid giving offence.

The locals are too polite to comment on your *faux pas*, but there are times when these normally phlegmatic people are roused to anger. In the cave temples at Dambulla, a photography ban was finally introduced after a tourist (certainly not the first) posed on the lap of a Buddha figure.

As there is a much more conservative moral code in Sri Lanka than in most Western countries, displays of affection in public are frowned upon – kissing and embracing usually take place behind umbrellas. Nudism is banned and going topless would be seen as insulting. It is, however, not uncommon to see men holding hands and embracing – a custom which is no more than an expression of friendship.

Sri Lankans never like to lose face in public. Patience and a smile generally achieve better results than angry words.

AYURVEDA

A medicine with a 3,000-year-old history now features in tour operators' catalogues as hotels along the southwest coast open up *ayurveda* clinics. Sri Lanka is one of the centres of this approach to health, which originated in India. About 10,000 doctors practise on the island and about a third of the population are among their patients.

Ayurveda may work where allopathic medicine fails, particularly on chronic or psychosomatic complaints such as rheumatism, skin disorders, high blood pressure, intestinal problems, respiratory diseases, migraines, asthma and diabetes.

According to *ayurvedic* philosophy the development of each person from birth is governed by the combination of five basic elements in nature – air, fire, water, earth and ether. Add to these three other classifications, *vatta*, *pitta* and *kapha*, and this is the starting point for Ayurvedic medicine. Any variations in these combined eight 'modalities' provide a basis for diagnosing and treating our individual health needs

Revitalisation therapy is a prominent feature of *ayurveda*; it is claimed that longevity without senile decay, heightened memory and improved bodily strength are all possible. *Ayurveda* is a holistic system, based on the idea that our well-being is closely related to our choice of lifestyle, habits and nourishment.

Below: ayurveda resort
Bottom: Kandyan flags

The Bandaranaike Clan

The Bandaranaike family, which has produced three prime ministers in the past 40 years, has played a large part in determining the fate of the country, but at great personal cost. The present state president, Chandrika Kumaratunga (born1945) lost her father at the hands of an assassin, and three decades later she lost her husband. Her father, Solomon Bandaranaike, shot by a monk before her eyes in 1959, had only been in office for three years.

The Sri Lankans then elected his widow, Sirimavo (1916–2000), as the world's first female head of state. 'Lady B' steered a radical socialist course on behalf of the Sri Lanka Freedom Party (SLFP), nationalising companies and tea plantations, introducing land reform, and distributing rice to the poor. Almost two decades of socialism (with interruptions up to 1977) brought major advances including a free health service.

In 1994 the Bandaranaikes made a spectacular comeback, with Sirimavo as prime minister and Chandrika as president. Chandrika was re-elected president in 1999. Her mother died in 2000 and was replaced as prime minister by Ratnasiri Wickremanayaka.

POLITICS AND ADMINISTRATION

The capital of the Democratic Socialist Republic of Sri Lanka is Colombo (pop. 1.6 million) with the seat of government in Sri Jayawardanapura, also known as Kotte. Elections are held every six years, but the country has not seen normal everyday politics for a long time as the conflict between Tamils and Sinhalese often finds expression in violence.

Both Sinhalese and Tamil politicians have been the targets for assassins. Two presidents, Solomon Bandaranaike (1959) and Ranasinghe Premadasa (1993), fell victim to the violence.

In the late 1970s, J.R. Jayawardene was an economically liberal, but authoritarian leader. He did, however, open up the country to the West. When in 1994 Chandrika Kumaratunga was elected president, young people and Tamils hoped she would bring the civil war to an end. She tried to reform the constitution and the administrative set-up in the provinces, with greater autonomy for the Tamils in the north and east (see pages 18–19), but was not able to fulfil hopes for peace.

THE ECONOMY

Sri Lanka's main exports are tea, rubber and coconut palm products. The plantation economy introduced under British rule had far-reaching consequences: a 'slash and burn' approach and the use, later on, of fertilisers and pesticides led to soil erosion and to dependence on food imports. Sri Lanka's agriculture is characterised by small, family-run concerns where rice, maize, millet and cassava are grown for personal consumption.

The creation of free trade zones was intended to speed up industrialisation but, despite low wages and tax and customs duty advantages, foreign investors stayed away, because of the civil war, unreliable power supplies and obsolete machinery. Only the garment industry now earns more foreign currency than the sale of tea.

Income from tourism, after a decade of civil war-related stagnation, is now increasing. The tourism industry employs 80,000 islanders.

The promising economic prognosis for the young and independent Ceylon after World War II did not materialise. Many years of a seemingly endless civil war have hindered progress. The infrastructure in the north and east is underdeveloped and an estimated 40 percent of the domestic budget is swallowed up by the war. Despite rising wages, most people earn less in real terms than they did 10 years ago. The price of a kilo of rice, for example, doubled in four years. Income per capita is around £350/US$240 a year.

One result of these poor economic conditions is that many children prostitute themselves on beaches. The government has taken some belated action and are now targeting foreign abusers who can expect a jail term of up to 20 years. Anonymous drop-in centres, a special police unit, raids and officials on the beach – though not any serious attempt to deal with the underlying economic causes – are just some of the measures adopted to bring an end to this exploitation.

The Free Trade Zones are another arena of abuse, this time of young female workers. Western clothing companies subcontract their manufacturing to factories where working conditions, pay and workers rights are pitiful. Needless to say, the profits flow to multinationals based in the West, not the local economy, as these companies pay poverty-level wages and little tax.

Top: warning notice
Middle: coconut seller
Bottom: bomb site, Jaffna

HISTORICAL HIGHLIGHTS

Prehistory Skeletons of Neanderthals have been found on the island.

483BC The Sinhalese under Prince Vijaya land and attack the original inhabitants. Vijaya becomes the island's first ruler.

393BC Anuradhapura becomes the capital of the kingdom.

250BC Mahinda, son of Ashoka, brings Buddhism to Sri Lanka, which soon becomes the state religion.

260BC Ashoka's daughter, Sangamitta, brings a cutting of the sacred Bo tree to Anuradhapura. During the next hundred years Tamils arrive from southern India and conquer Anuradhapura.

161BC King Dutthagamani defeats the Tamils. During the following centuries Sri Lanka is a united kingdom. Achievements include the construction of reservoirs, canals, palaces and dagobas.

In the first millennium AD Repeated invasions by Tamils, with power regularly changing hands. In 993 Anuradhapura is taken by the South Indian Cholas. The seat of government moves to Polonnaruwa, which remains the Sinhalese capital for over two centuries, Tamils rule the whole of Sri Lanka for 80 years.

1070 King Vijayabahu succeeds in driving out the Cholas.

13th century Sinhalese empire collapses due to power struggles within the Sinhalese monarchy and threats from outside. Polonnaruwa is abandoned and the Tamils found the kingdom of Eelam in the north. Parakramabahu VI unifies the island briefly. On his death, it fragments into three kingdoms: Kotte and Kandy (both Sinhalese) and Jaffna (Tamil).

1505 The Portuguese arrive attracted by Sri Lanka's favourable position on trade routes. Cinnamon becomes a valuable commodity. As the islanders are converted to Christianity, countless temples are destroyed and Buddhist monks driven out.

1636 The Kandyan kingdom forms an alliance with the Dutch who had ousted the Portuguese from the east coast. Some 20 years later, Dutch troops conquer Colombo and take control of the coast.

1658–1796 Dutch colonial rule in Ceylon continues and large areas of the island become cinnamon plantations.

1796 The Dutch give way to the British, who bring Indian officials to the island. Their presence leads to disputes between Indians and Sinhalese.

1815 British troops defeat the Kandyan king and for the first time the whole island falls under foreign rule. The British build roads and railways, and introduce a Western education system. English becomes the official language.

1832 Changes in property laws favour British settlers at the expense of the Sinhalese. Spread of coffee, cinnamon and coconut plantations.

1867 The first field of tea is planted near Kandy, and railways reach the plantations. Tea becomes a profitable export.

1886 Ruins of Polonnaruwa discovered.

1931 Universal adult suffrage introduced.

4 February 1948 Ceylon achieves independence. D.S. Senanayake of the United Nationalist Party (UNP) becomes the first prime minister. The British monarch remains head of state.

1956 The UNP is defeated and Solomon Bandaranaike of the Sri Lanka Freedom Party (SLFP) becomes prime minister. Sinhalese becomes the official language. Sinhalese nationalism, tinged with elements of Buddhism and socialism, intensifies ethnic conflict.

1959 S. Bankaranaike is assassinated.

1960 Sirimavo Bandaranaike, his widow, becomes the world's first woman prime minister and continues to promote Sinhalese nationalist policies.

1965 Mrs Bandaranaike is defeated and Dudley Senananyake of the UNP becomes prime minister.

1966 Poya days become public holidays.

1970 Mrs Bandaranaike is returned to power and introduces measures to extend nationalisation, reduce social inequality and achieve land reform.

1972 'Ceylon' is officially renamed Sri Lanka and a republican constitution is adopted. The Tamil Tigers take up arms in support of an autonomous region in the northeast of the island.

1977 Landslide victory of J.R. Jayawardene in the prime ministerial elections brings economic 'liberalisation'.

1978 A new constitution introduces proportional representation and the office of president. J.R. Jayawardene of the UNP becomes the first president.

1983 Simmering discontent boils over into a Tigers' attack on the army in Jaffna. The incident sparks ethnic clashes and the intensification of separatist guerrilla activity.

1987 Indian troops arrive on Sri Lanka to help suppress the Tamil rebels.

1989 Ranasinghe Premadasa (UNP) is elected president.

1990s Indian troops leave Sri Lanka. The Tamil Tigers take control in the north and assassinate high-ranking military officers and politicians, including the Indian prime minister, Rajiv Gandhi (1991), and president Premadasa (1993).

1994 Chandrika Kumuratunga of the SLFP (Sri Lanka Freedom Party) is elected as president. Her mother, Sirima Bandaranaike, becomes prime minister. Negotiations with the LTTE begin.

1995 Peace talks with LTTE representatives break down after a series of explosions caused by the Tamil rebels.

1996 Massive bomb attacks shake Colombo's business quarter. Sri Lanka's cricket team wins the Word Cup.

1997 The largest opposition party and LTTE reject the federation plan. In October a bomb devastates Colombo. Constitutional reforms to end the civil war are tabled, with regional reform intended to give the Tamils greater autonomy.

1998 Peace talks suffer another setback. Sixteen people are killed by a bomb in Kandy. The proposed constitutional reform is rejected by the opposition.

1999 Chandrika Kumaratunga survives an assassination attempt and is re-elected president in December.

2000 Sirimavo Bandaranaike dies, Ratnasiri Wickremanayaka becomes prime minister. Tigers capture Elephant Pass, their biggest victory to date, and declare a unilateral ceasefire.

2001 The government rejects the ceasefire and launches a major attack on the rebels' positions.

Map
on page
30

*Previous pages: reclining
Buddha, Anuradhapura
Below: Kathiresan Kovil, detail
Bottom: Pettah Mosque*

1: Colombo

Colombo's hotchpotch of fine Victorian buildings, grey concrete blocks and rickety wooden shacks is not a sprawling giant like many Asian cities. The atmosphere is generally leisurely in true Asian style – except on the streets. Colourful trishaws (three-wheel taxis) jostle with the countless privately owned minibuses – an alarming combination during the rush hour and one that leaves a veil of pollution over the city.

But there is something captivating about the port city of Colombo. Exotic smells emanate from roadside stalls – some whet the appetite, some, particularly in the bazaar quarter, are less appealing. Nowhere else do so many jeans and loose white shirts merge with bright saris and orange-coloured monks' habits. Nowhere else do Buddhist and Hindu temples, churches and mosques co-exist side by side in such profusion, oases of calm amid the hustle and bustle of the capital.

SEAFARING TOWN

Seafarers have been dropping anchor off Colombo for thousands of years, but the earliest written mention of the port may be that of Fa-hsien, the 5th-century Chinese traveller, who referred to it as Kao-lan-pu. The Sinhalese called the port Kolamba, which the Portuguese thought was derived from the Sinhalese word for mango trees. But *kolamba* was also an old Sinhalese word meaning 'port' or 'ferry'.

In the 8th century AD, Arab merchants settled near the site of the modern port and began trading with the Sinhalese kingdom based in nearby Kotte (also the sight of modern-day Sri Lanka's parliament). The Portuguese (from 1505) and the Dutch (from 1658) built houses and a fort, but the most obvious visible signs of the city's colonial past were left here by the British who took control at the end of the 18th century. Colombo became the island's capital in 1815, after the Sinhalese chiefs deposed the king of Kandy and ceded his territory to the British.

SIGHTS

The oldest districts of the city, near the harbour and north of Beira Lake, are known as Fort and the Pettah ('the city outside the fort'). The ★★ **Fort District**, by the harbour, is the city's commercial hub, while the ★★★ **Pettah** is the bazaar quarter. Situated to the south of Beira Lake is the Southern Quarter, which includes the built-up area of Cinnamon Gardens, a region important for its cinnamon growing during the Dutch period.

FORT DISTRICT

Unfortunately the remains of the fort cannot be seen. The medieval fortress is now the police and naval headquarters, and military checkpoints block access to the old ruins.

Begin your tour of the district by its best-known landmark, the ★ **Lighthouse Clock Tower ❶**. Built in 1857, it was used for many years as a lighthouse – the only one in the world that also told the time in the middle of a busy street – but was later replaced by a more modern one on Marine Drive. Banks, travel agencies, telephone shops, barbers, jewellers and small restaurants line **Chatham Street ❷** – a mixture of the old-style Asian and the new. Bank employees rub shoulders with street traders and beggars.

Star Attractions
- **Fort District**
- **The Pettah**

Street Names
Colombo's streets are supposed to be signposted in Sinhalese, Tamil and English. However, it may be better to look on shopfronts to find out what the current name of the street is. Many of the old English street names have been changed to express a more Sri Lankan identity. Thus, Parsons Road has become Sir Chittampalam Gardiner Mawatha, and Flower Road is now Sir Ernest de Silva Mawatha.

The jewellers' bazaar

Map below

OLD AND MODERN FACADES

Towering above the colonial facades and mosque towers in Fort are the symbols of the modern age. Two mirror-glazed, circular multi-storey giants housing the **World Trade Centre** and the **Bank of Ceylon** gleam in the sun as vanguards of an expanding skyline.

In the two-storey state-owned **Laksala Craft Centre ❸** in York Street, you will find a veritable treasure trove of wooden carvings and batiks, brassware and basketwork, jewellery and children's toys, all sold at fixed prices.

Historic store

If you prefer to haggle with street traders, you should first have a good look at prices and quality here. Only then will you come away with a bargain when you strike a deal on the street.

Cargill's ❹, built in 1845, sells everything from toothpaste to road maps and umbrellas. This is the oldest department store in Sri Lanka, its red facade pointing the way to the harbour.

For security reasons the harbour region can be viewed only from an elevated position, possibly

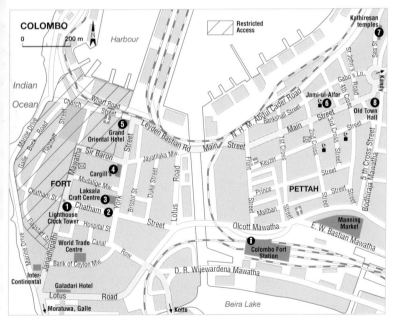

the Harbour Room Restaurant on the 4th floor of the **Grand Oriental Hotel ❺**, one of the classic colonial buildings, built in the 1850s originally as a barracks for soldiers, but then converted into a hotel and refurbished in 1991.

THE PETTAH

It is impossible to miss the bazaar quarter – from Fort follow Main Street, cross the canal, keeping with the crowds. People, animals and vehicles push and jostle through the streets and alleys of the old market quarter, where loading and unloading never seems to end.

Vendors stand on tables amid their wares and customers, throwing underwear and saris up into the air, extolling their quality in a loud singsong, while clapping their hands and tap-dancing on the spot, physically attracting customers' attention. Porters lug thick bundles of timber, half-naked men run along 5th Cross Street pulling dangerously overloaded carts, a lottery ticket seller accosts passers-by with a megaphone. A deafening and breathtaking experience, the Pettah is dusty, colourful and smells strongly of fish.

The mosque in 2nd Cross Street is the striking ★ **Jami-ul-Alfar ❻** with its red and white minarets and columns. Otherwise known as the Pettah Mosque, it is closed to the public while prayers are being said.

TRADING PLACES

As is common in bazaar districts all over South Asia, the roads in the Pettah are divided up according to various trades. Electrical equipment in one, textiles or vegetables in another.

If you follow the more attractive smells in the Pettah, then you will be drawn by the aroma of herbs in **Gabo's Lane**, where *ayurveda* shops, who can advise you on what to take, sell their natural medicines from baskets and sacks. **Sea Street** is crammed with an array of small jewellers and goldsmiths, very popular with Sri Lankans and Indians – especially brides to be.

The British Legacy
Even if many of the old English street names have now disappeared, there is still a fine array of colonial architecture to be seen. Sir D.B. Jayatilleke Mawatha is lined by a number of imposing buildings. Particular gems elsewhere include the Grand Oriental Hotel, dating from the 1850s, the Old Town Hall, built in 1873, and the Lighthouse Clock Tower, built in 1857.

Street trader, Pettah

Of all the Hindu temples in the market quarter, it is worth taking a look at the ancient and new **Kathiresan temples ⑦** in Sea Street. The complex is dedicated to Skanda. When the Hindus celebrate the *Vel* Festival *(see page 93)*, this is where the procession starts. Skanda's weapons are carried through the street on a decorated ox cart.

On the way to Sea Street, on Bodhiraja Mawatha, is the **Old Town Hall ⑧**. Built in 1873, it has been extensively restored and retains the double portico which once gave access to horse-drawn carriages. It is still used as municipal offices, and on the first floor you can see the meeting room where costumed mannequins recreate a 1906 meeting of town councillors. The adjoining **Colombo Municipal Council Museum** has some fascinating exhibits relating to local history.

Kathiresan Kovil

GALLE FACE GREEN

For a relaxing and refreshing afternoon tea, try the ★ **Galle Face Hotel ⑨**, built in 1864. Seated in a wicker armchair on the veranda, gazing out over the ocean and being served by a waiter in a long white sarong, it is easy to imagine that time has stood still. Rockefeller and Gregory Peck both fell in love with the hotel's terrace. The hotel is situated at the end of the **Galle Face Green** esplanade beside the Indian Ocean. In the evening this open space, recently restored to its original splendour as a green lawn, swarms with families, young courting couples and joggers. Appetising smells waft across from the food stalls, children fly kites and boys play cricket.

THE SOUTHERN QUARTER

The snow-white **Devatagaha Mosque ⑩**, situated near the **New Town Hall** by De Soysa Circus in the south of Colombo, is one of the city's oldest Muslim prayer halls, built more than a century ago. Its numerous towers and minarets could well have been an inspiration for Walt Disney.

The nearby ★★ **National Museum** ⑪ in the smart Cinnamon Gardens district – actually there is now only one cinnamon tree left – is worth a visit if you are not planning a detour to the royal cities of the 'Cultural Triangle'. The two-storey museum offers a fascinating insight into Sri Lankan history and its ancient crafts (8 Sir Marcus Fernando Mawatha, Colombo 7, tel: 694 7678; daily 9am–5pm, closed Friday and public holidays).

The museum forms the nucleus of a complex of cultural institutions, all of which are in the well-maintained Viharamahadevi Park. The other museums found here are the **National History Museum** and the **National Art Gallery**, which, in addition to its permanent collection of works by Sri Lankan artists, holds temporary exhibitions of contemporary art. The park itself has a wide selection of plants and trees, and the official gardeners give an interesting tour of its flora.

South of the park, on Guildford Crescent, is the **Lionel Wendt Theatre and Art Gallery**. This is the most important of Colombo's venues for the performing arts, particularly music. Exhibitions of contemporary arts and crafts are also held here.

Some fine examples of old churches line Galle Road. The Anglican **St Andrew's Church** ⑫, next to the Lanka Oberoi hotel, is one of the most interesting.

Star Attraction
●National Museum

Museum Highlights
Among the many treasures in the National Museum, perhaps the star exhibit (in Gallery 8) is the throne, crown and footstool of the Kandyan kings. The jewel-encrusted artefacts, made for King Rajasinghe I (1636–87), were appropriated by the British and made their way to Windsor Castle, where they remained until they were returned to Sri Lanka in 1934. Gallery 2 has a fine collection of moonstones, while Gallery 4 has representations of Hindu deities and a number of 12th-century Chinese bowls found during excavations at Polonnaruwa.

Kandyan performers

Map on page 32

EXCURSIONS FROM COLOMBO

The ★ **Raja Maha Vihara** in Kelaniya, about 10km (7 miles) north of the city centre, is certainly worth a visit, ideally at the weekend. That is when the inhabitants of Colombo find time to pay their respects to the Buddha with flowers, oil lamps and drum rhythms. This Buddhist temple is said to have been built in the 5th century BC and was apparently visited by the Buddha himself, who preached to warring factions of the futility of conflict. The complex, therefore, is one of the most important on the island.

During the course of the past 800 years, the shrine has been repeatedly destroyed: first, before the 13th century, by a Tamil king, and later, during the 16th century, by the missionary zeal of the Portuguese. Reconstruction began about a hundred years ago and at the January full moon in every year since 1927 the *Duruthu perahera* (procession in honour of the Buddha) has started here. The site consists of an extraordinary white doorway and a *dagoba* (relic chamber), a richly decorated prayer house and a huge Bo tree.

Inside the temple are a series of paintings depicting episodes in the life of the Buddha, large statues and ceiling paintings. Bus no. 235 goes to the temple from the Pettah, while a three-wheel taxi will cost about Rs 150.

Below: a detail from Raja Maha Vihara
Bottom: visiting the temple

DEHIWALA

The small **Dehiwala Zoo** (daily 8am–6pm), at Dehiwala to the south of Colombo, has an enclosure for wild cats and various other predatory animals, as well as a collection of many colourful and exotic birds. It is situated on Dharmapal Mawatha, off Galle Road.

The zoo pioneered the practice of placing animals in large, landscaped enclosures – rather than locking them up in cages – and the animals seem happier than they might do in some other South Asian zoos. However, the whole concept of a zoo is distasteful to many people and some visitors might be put off by the performing elephant show that takes place every afternoon.

2: Kandy

Nestling in pleasantly cool hill country in a bend in the River Mahaweli and by an attractive lake lies Sri Lanka's third-largest town and guardian of the country's finest Buddhist treasure, a tooth from the mouth of the Buddha himself. Morning and evening, when drums proclaim the opening of the famous shrine, the area outside becomes a frenzy of activity as the pilgrims pray, the monks beg and the tourists click away, but the tooth itself is something only the chosen few see.

Kandy has always been the spiritual centre of Sri Lanka. According to legend, Princess Hemamala brought the tooth of the Buddha here hidden in her hair almost 1,700 years ago. The relic is accorded the highest possible status throughout the island.

Kandy arose as a haven for Sinhalese fleeing conflict elsewhere on the island. Its remote jungle loction helped it maintain its status as the last independent state in Sri Lanka. It held out against European invaders for over two centuries, finally falling to the British in 1815. A fascinating account of the life of the city was written by the British sailor, Robert Knox, who was held prisoner there in the 17th century. He was captured in 1660 and spent the next 19½ years as a 'guest' of the Kandyan king, Rajasinha II.

Map on page 36

Protective Relic
It is believed that as long as the sacred tooth resides in the temple ar Kandy and the rituals of the annual *perahera* are performed correctly, the country will not suffer from famine, revolution or calamity.

Shrine of the Tooth

Map below

BY KANDY LAKE

The city's main attraction is the ★★★ **Dalada Maligawa ❶**, the Temple of the Tooth, situated beside the lake. Several times a day the holy shrine is opened for the *puja (see page 89)*, when the faithful and tourists throng past the shrine. Buddhists get down on their knees out of respect, and with mountains of aralia and lotus blossom piled high on the altar, oboe players and drummers accompany the ceremony on historic instruments. The tooth itself is heavily guarded; mere mortals are only allowed to see the outside of

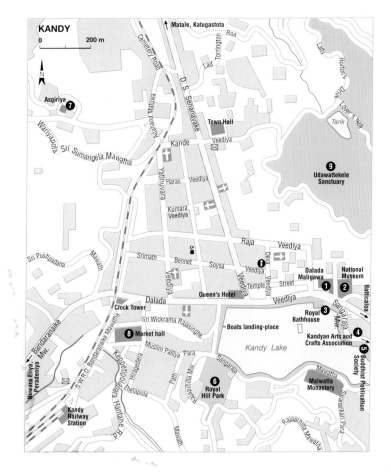

KANDY

0   200 m

N

Matale, Katugastota

Asgiriya ❼

Warivapola Sri Sumangela Mawatha

Cemetery Road

Rajapihilla Mawatha

D. S. Senanayake

Lad Torrington Road

Lady Horton's Drive

Lover's Walk

Tank

Town Hall

Kande Veediya

Yatinuvara

Haras Veediya

Udawattekele Sanctuary ❾

Kumara Veediya

Sri Pushpadana

Mawath

Srimath

Bennet

Soysa

Raja Veediya

Dela Veediya

Veediya

Temple Street

Dalada Maligawa ❶

National Museum ❷

Batticaloa

Queen's Hotel

Dalada Veediya

Clock Tower

Sri Wickrama Rajasinghe

Market hall ❽

Muslim Palliya Para

Boats landing-place

Royal Bathhouse ❸

Kandyan Arts and Crafts Association ❹

Buddhist Publication Society ❺

Sangaraja Mw.

Bandaranaike Mw.

Nuwara Eliya Peradeniya

S.W.R.D. Bandaranaike Mawatha

Keppetipola Ehelapola

Hirapedera

Pitti

Sangarala

Kandy Lake

Malwatta Monastery

Mawatha

Smanakkari Para

Royal Hill Park ❻

Kandy Railway Station

Rajapihilla Mawatha

the seven precious casks shaped in the form of a *dagoba* – and then through bullet-proof glass. *Pujas* begin at 5.30am, 9.30am and 6.30pm.

The shrine is then open for one to two hours, although the temple itself with its ceiling paintings, ivory carvings, the Buddha made from rock crystal and the library with palm-leaf manuscripts is open for the rest of the day.

THE BUDDHA'S TOOTH

The Buddha's tooth has had an exciting history. It was initially protected by the kingdom of Kalinga in India. With the resurgence of Hinduism, King Guhasiva feared for its safety and hid it in his daughter Hemamala's hair, who then took it to Sri Lanka. It passed through various rulers' hands until it was captured by South Indian raiders around the 13th century. King Parakrama of Polonnaruwa recaptured it from the Tamils and assigned a special bodyguard to protect it.

The tooth was next abducted by the Portuguese in the 16th century. They took it to Goa, where they tried to destroy it. However, it is said the tooth escaped and flew back to Sri Lanka. It was last captured by the British when they took Kandy in 1815. They opened the sacred caskets and did indeed find a tooth within them, albeit one that was 5cm in length. Since then, the tooth has remained in the Dalada Maligawa as one of the most sacred objects of the Buddhist world.

AROUND KANDY

Situated next to the temple is the ★★ **National Museum ❷** (daily 9am–5pm, closed Friday), where jewellery, pottery, fabrics and weaponry from the Kandyan kingdom are exhibited. In the former **Royal Bathhouse ❸** by the lake a 15-minute video details the history of Kandy (daily 9am–4.30pm, closed Friday). Available here are permits for the 'Cultural Triangle' *(see page 41).*

If you feel in the mood for a walk, then a footpath (4km/2½ miles) follows the shores of the man-made lake, which dates from 1807. On the

Star Attractions
● **Dalada Maligawa**
● **National Museum**

Temple Etiquette
Non-Buddhist visitors are allowed into the Temple of the Tooth but it is essential they observe certain rules. They must be dressed modestly and covered up (long sleeves and skirts or trousers), remove their shoes and walk barefoot in the temple precincts, and walk clockwise around the shrines. It is considered offensive to sit with the soles of your feet facing the Buddha or a Buddhist monk.

Opposite: Inner Sanctum door, detail
Below: Temple of the Tooth and Royal Bath House.

Map
on page
36

way snake charmers, balloon sellers, beggars and clowns try their luck with the tourists in the hope of picking up a few rupees.

ARTS AND CRAFTS

By the shore a few hundred metres to the east is the **Kandyan Arts and Crafts Association** ❹ where carpet weavers and craftsmen display their skills (daily 9am–12.30pm and 1–5pm). The crafts they produce make good souvenirs and can be bought next door.

At the eastern end of the lake a bookshop belonging to the **Buddhist Publication Society** ❺ sells multilingual Buddhist literature. The society staff here can give advice on meditation courses (54 Sangaraja Mawatha; open Monday to Friday 8.30–4pm, Saturday 9.30am–noon).

> **Dance Performances**
> If you are spending some time in Kandy then you should try to get to one of the dance performances. Kandyan dancers usually perform from 7.30pm on a number of different stages, for example in the Lake Club (tickets from the Queen's Hotel) and in the Kandy Dance Show Hall near the Kandyan Arts and Crafts Association.

MARKETS AND PARKS

Pass Kandy's oldest monastery, **Malwatta**, and you eventually reach the corner of the lake and **Royal Hill Park** ❻. After a half-hour walk up a hill you can enjoy a magnificent panoramic view of the city that also takes in the giant-sized white Buddha in **Asgiriya** ❼ in the north, a feature of the second most important monastery in Kandy.

On the western bank boats wait to take trippers around the small island in the middle of the lake. It is not far from here to the covered street markets and the two-storey **market hall** ❽ with many colourful fruit, vegetable and spice stalls (daily 6am–7pm).

It's worth pausing between sightseeing trips to experience the natural beauty of the **Udawattekele Sanctuary** ❾. A dense canopy of leaves covering a wide range of exotic flora absorbs the din of horns and engines from the city. Fauna includes a wealth of bird and insect life, not to mention a good few monkeys. If you are visiting the sanctuary during the rainy season, wear sturdy ankle-high shoes to protect against leeches (the walk is around 5km/3miles and the park entrance is at the end of Kande Veediya; daily 8am–5pm).

Lacquer-work craftsman

DAY TRIPS

A whole day quickly passes in the ★★ **Botanical Gardens** in Peradeniya, which were originally laid out in 1371. Flourishing in an area of about 60 hectares (150 acres) are more than 5,000 plant species. You can walk through palm avenues and admire the giant trees. Delicate flowers blossom in the orchid house, while in the spice garden an intense aroma pervades the air. Peradeniya is situated 6km (4 miles) from the city centre and can be reached by bus (daily 7.30am–5pm).

TEMPLE SITES

If you fancy a lengthy walk, then you can cover the three oldest temples in the Kandy district in a day. The best starting point is the **Gadaladeniya Temple** (trishaw, bus from Peradeniya, about 6km/4 miles). In this 600-year-old Buddhist complex, the Buddha and the Hindu gods, Shiva and Vishnu, appear in the form of frescoes and statues.

From here continue in a southerly direction through palm and bamboo groves, past tea plantations and shops selling brassware until you can see the light blue ★ **Lankatilaka Temple** on the rock (about 4km/2½ miles). The inside of this imposing sanctuary (1344) has several shrines, from which the Hindu gods, Vishnu, Skanda and Ganesh, survey the visitors.

Star Attraction
● **Botanical Gardens**

Below: in the Botanical Gardens
Bottom: Lankatilaka Temple

Map on page 42

Sri Lanka's Elephants

Sadly, Sri Lanka's wild elephant population is in decline. Outside of the wildlife sanctuaries, visitors are most likely to encounter elephants working with their *mahouts*, either carrying heavy loads of timber, giving rides to tourists or, most spectacularly, decorated and taking part in *perahera* processions. One of the most famous is the annual procession in Kandy, where a 'tusker' carries a replica of the casket which hold the sacred tooth, followed by 12 other richly decorated elephants.

Embekke Temple, detail

An uneven path continues southwards past a quarry where women earn Rs 20 for breaking stones – and their working practices have probably changed little since the 600-year-old ★ **Embekke Temple** (2km/1¼ miles) was built. The main attraction here is the superbly maintained carvings from the 14th century on the columns in the Drummers' Hall. The finest of the 500 or so figures are the dancer, a double-headed eagle, the swans and the soldiers. A bus leaves at irregular intervals from Embekke. If you do not want to walk, the temple can also be visited directly from Kandy by trishaw (2–3 hours).

ANCIENT CITADEL

Lying in the mountains 35km (22 miles) to the east of the city is the well-protected citadel of **Hunnasgiriya**. This is where the kings and populace of Kandy, taking with them the sacred tooth, would retire to when the city was threatened by invaders.

On the top of the mountain are the ruins of **Medamahanuwara**, the city where the people would take refuge. The views are spectacular.

ELEPHANT ORPHANAGE

If you are fascinated by elephants, then you simply must go to Pinnawela. In the ★ **Elephant Orphanage** you are first given a short introduction to the life of a domesticated elephant.

About 60 pachyderms, both large and small, are fed, pampered and taken to water beside the River Kuda-Oya, where many a tourist has been on the receiving end of a trunkful of water. The orphanage, the only one of its kind in the world, was founded in 1975 to raise abandoned baby elephants.

The 40-km (25-mile) journey from Kandy to the elephant orphanage takes 1–2 hours by bus (trishaw costs about Rs 500, taxi about Rs 1,500). Feeding times daily at 9.15am, 1.15am and 5pm; bath times 10am–noon. The sanctuary is open daily 8am–5pm.

3: The Cultural Triangle

Colombo – Negombo – Anuradhapura – Mihintale – Polonnaruwa – Sigiriya – Dambulla – Nalanda Gedige – Aluvihara – Kandy (521km/321 miles)

Map on page 42

You need at least three days, or better a whole week, to explore the so-called 'Cultural Triangle', the region where much of the country's 2,000-year-old heritage is found. Among the historic royal towns with their countless palaces and temple ruins lie ancient cave monasteries and some of the finest and largest Buddha statues on the island. Man-made 'tanks' (artifical lakes) and canals testify to the engineering and irrigation skills of the islanders' forebears.

Anyone who climbs the Lion Rock in Sigiriya and sees the view over the jungle from 200m (650ft) will surely envy King Kasyapa his lofty residence, which dates from the 5th century.

HEADING NORTH

The fishing and tourist town of ★ **Negombo** is the ideal place to relax for the first few days of your stay, as it is only a few kilometres from the airport. There are a number of attractive places along the southwest coast and north of Negombo, if you want to make the most of the beaches.

Below: Sigiriya mural
Bottom: Negombo

Map below

Negombo is famous for its unusual catamarans *(oruwa)* with three-piece sails and for its system of canals. During the 17th century, the Dutch built a waterway to Colombo from Puttalam 100km (60 miles) to the north to transport the precious spices. A boat trip into the lagoon or out to sea is a pleasant way of spending an afternoon.

A lot of visitors like to tour the small town by bike, in which case the best place to start would be the **fish market**, where the freshly landed fish

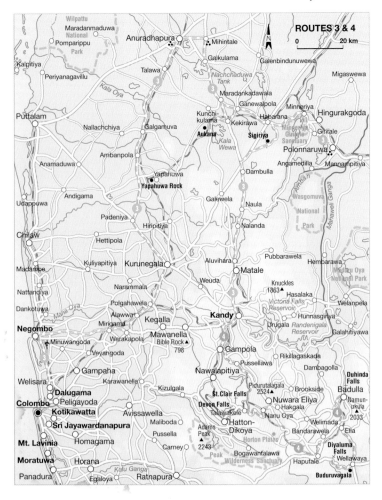

and seafood are sold. Many of the fishermen live in wretched huts made from plastic sheets and corrugated iron – not next to, but right in the middle of a rubbish tip. The contrast with the northern part of the town could not be greater. On or off Lewis Place, there are lots of guesthouses, hotels, garden restaurants and souvenir shops.

INTO THE TRIANGLE

The route into the interior runs past countless coconut plantations. In one factory you can see how all the produce that the palm tree offers is manufactured *(see page 14)*. The gateway to the 'Cultural Triangle' is **Kurunegala**, a royal town dating from the 13th century, but only a few ruins remain.

A visit to ★ **Yapahuwa** is of interest to those with an interest in archaeology. Briefly during the 13th century, the rock fortress was the island's capital. A flight of steps and a stone portal with richly decorated ornaments and columns are all that have survived.

ANURADHAPURA

During the 4th century BC the small settlement here was the first of Sri Lanka's royal towns. This was where the rulers started building the system of reservoirs and irrigation canals *(see page 51)*. Nuwara Wewa, Tissa Wewa, Basawak Kulam and Bulan Kulam are the names of the large artificial lakes (or 'tanks' as the British colonials called them) in ★★★ **Anuradhapura**. Their function was to turn the Dry Zone into an important agricultural region. It has also become a habitat for rare herons and other bird species.

In 993 the Tamils plundered the site and burned it to the ground, leaving nothing but devastation. The jungle slowly moved in on the abandoned ruins of the royal palaces and *dagobas*. At the end of the 19th century the British started to excavate the archaeological treasures. The work was continued with UNESCO's assistance.

The 20-sq km (8-sq mile) wide area of ruins (206km/128 miles northeast of Colombo) will

Star Attraction
● Anuradhapura

Oruwas
These distinctive dugout fishing canoes with outriggers can be traced back to the 1st century, when they were mentioned by the Roman historian Pliny. It is thought the design of the canoes had arrived much earlier, either from traders from the Comoros Islands close to Mozambique, or from peoples of the Pacific.

Below: Anuradhapura, detail
Bottom: the Buddha's footprint

Ruvanveliseya Dagoba

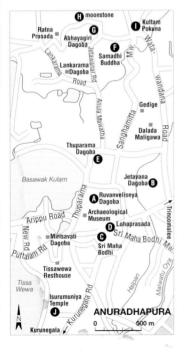

challenge even experienced walkers. It is a better idea to hire a bicycle or to negotiate with a hire car or trishaw driver.

Amateur archaeologists would find much of interest here. Even three days would barely be enough. The atmosphere is particularly moving during the full moon festival in June when thousands of pilgrims flock to the site.

SOUTHERN SECTION

Following its restoration, the ★★★ **Ruvanveliseya Dagoba Ⓐ** with its gilded spire, is now gleaming white. Work started on the temple in 144BC during the reign of King Dutthagamani. According to Buddhist mythology, elephants have the task of supporting the earth, thus explaining the many striking elephant sculptures around the platform.

There is always a hive of activity by the ★ **Jetavana Dagoba Ⓑ**. Restoration work has been going on here for years. Women workers skilfully balance bricks on their heads as they work on the restoration of the shrine to its original height of about 120m (400ft).

Thousands of Buddhists come to make offerings underneath the ★★ **Sri Maha Bodhi Ⓒ**, the oldest historically authenticated tree in the world and one of the holiest Buddhist sites. People are attracted because this fine specimen originated from the tree under which the Buddha sat to attain enlightenment in Bodhgaya in India 2,500 years ago. It is said that 200 years later the Indian princess, Sanghamitta, brought the sapling over and transplanted it here. Most of the island's other Bo trees came from this source.

A golden railing, often swathed in colourful prayer flags, surrounds the giant tree. On *poya* (full moon) days every month pilgrims throng round the tree, honouring the Buddha with chanting and gifts. It is a rare sight to see the shaven-headed Buddhist nuns in white robes who gather here.

Not far away stands a forest of columns that once supported the ★ **Lohaprasada** , the Brazen Palace (named after the now-disappeared roof, reputedly made from bronze). Once a nine-storey structure, this would have been the heart of monastic life in the city.

The oldest Buddhist building on the island is the small 3rd-century BC ★ **Thuparama Dagoba** **E**. It has been restored on a number of occasions, but was originally commissioned by King Tissa to house the Buddha's right collarbone.

NORTHERN SECTION

Cycle or drive to the north of the excavation site. The **Samadhi Buddha** **F** has meditated here since the 4th century AD, while the **Abhayagiri Dagoba** **G** was once the centre of a monastery, the confines of which contained the remarkably well-preserved **moonstone** **H** *(see page 83)* at the threshold of the **Mahasena Palace**.

The monks' pools, **Kuttam Pokuna** or **Twin Ponds** **I**, are a masterpiece of Sinhalese water engineering and masonry work.

Don't miss the chance to visit the ★ **Isurumuniya Temple** **J**. Of special interest are the stone reliefs, including the playful elephants on the rock above the pond and the graceful 'Isurumuniya Lovers' in the museum.

Star Attractions
● Ruvanveliseya Dagoba
● Sri Maha Bodhi

> 👁 *Dagobas*
> These hemispherical structures were built to contain relics of the Buddha or other holy people. Initally they took the form of a mound of earth. Later the design developed into the masonry *stupas* of India, *chedis* of Thailand and *dagobas* of Sri Lanka. There are many of them dotted across the Sri Lankan landscape, the most impressive of which were built by the kings of Anuradhapura. In their most common form they consist of a dome standing on a square base, topped with a pinnacle.

Isurumuniya temple

Map on page 42

Birds and Beasts
Birding enthusiasts will almost certainly want to stay longer in this region. **Giritale** and **Minneriya** tanks are part of a nature reserve where rare species of heron, kingfishers and many other feathered exotica can be observed. Around **Habarana**, it is not uncommon for lone, wild elephants to emerge from the jungle to graze close to the road.

Aukana Buddha

CRADLE OF CEYLONESE BUDDHISM

The atmosphere surrounding ★★ **Mihintale**, the 'cradle of Ceylonese Buddhism', is always calm and peaceful, particularly at sunset. From the top of the sacred hill a splendid view extends over the broad plain, the Anuradhapura *dagobas* silhouetted in the distance. While on a hunting trip here in 247BC, King Devanampiyatissa was converted to Buddhism after encountering the great Indian sage Mahinda. Following his conversion, the new religion spread rapidly across the island.

If you are not worn out after climbing the 1,840 steps to the plateau, you can continue up the **Sila Rock**. It is steep and winding but the panoramic view from the top is stunning. Every year in June during the *poya* festival, thousands of Buddhist pilgrims make their way to this sacred place. The complex comprises several dagobas, a monastery, the smooth slab of stone known as Mahinda's Bed, an outsized Buddha and Sinha Pokuna or the Lion Bath.

Off the tourist route and reached by crossing the Kala Wewa embankment, ★ **Aukana Buddha** blesses his imaginary flock. The 13-m (40-ft) high, truly imposing statue is said to have been hewn from the rock in the 5th century.

After all this, you might feel like a few days' rest from sightseeing, and several resort complexes with chalets, swimming pool and every imaginable comfort are situated between Anuradhapura and Polonnaruwa.

NORTHERN CENTRAL PROVINCE

Many exiles from the northeast live in the region between Anuradhapura and Polonnaruwa. The invisible border with the Tamil region runs through here. It is impossible to miss the military posts and checkpoints behind piles of sandbags and car tyres, where soldiers can safely check the papers of civilian travellers.

By the roadside you will see families of dummies made from straw standing in front of their farmhouse on stilts waving. The message they are conveying is 'tourists are welcome here'.

POLONNARUWA

The second royal city is ★★★ **Polonnaruwa**. One of the last Sinhalese kings to reign here during the 12th century was Parakramabahu, a far-sighted monarch who extended the existing canals and lakes and laid the foundations for a modern irrigation system. In 1314, Polonnaruwa was abandoned because of continuing attacks by Tamils from the north.

Cycles can be rented to explore this ancient site 360km (216 miles) from Colombo. Many buildings and archaeological treasures are still hidden by jungle growth.

Star Attractions
- Mihintale
- Polonnaruwa
- Thuparama Image House

INSIDE THE CITY WALL

Walk through the small chambers of Parakramabahu's ★ **Royal Palace** Ⓐ and you will see that this brick structure built 700 years ago consisted of several floors, probably seven.

Only a few metres away lie the ★ **Audience Hall** Ⓑ and the ★ **Royal Bath** Ⓒ. The assembly hall is decorated with moonstones, relief elephants and *makara* figures, mythical dragon-like creatures. A stone flight of steps climbs up to the Royal Bath. Underground pipes brought fresh water from the nearby pond to the square pool.

A few hundred metres further north are many well-preserved ruins. The ★★ **Thuparama**

Below: relief of a lion
Bottom: Thuparama
Image House

POLONNARUWA

0   300 m

Tivanka
Image House
(Jetavana) **N**

Lotus Pond **M**

Gal
Vihara **L**

Kiri
Vihara **J K**
Lankatilaka
Image House

Giritale

Rankoth Vihara **I**

Satmahal
Prasada **H**
Atadage **G F** Hatadage Temple
Parakrama
E Vatadage
Samudra
D Circular Temple
Thuparama
image house
B Audience Hall
Royal Palace
A Royal Bath
Resthouse

Rock sculpture
Potgul Vihara **P**

Batticaloa

Historical   City Wall

Image House D dating from the 12th century is one of the best of Polonnaruwa's surviving treasures – for one thing, it's the only one with a roof. The outer walls are covered with bas-reliefs.

The oldest and probably most unusual building is the ★★★ **Vatadage Circular Temple E**. The ornate reliefs were clearly the work of master stonemasons. Note the fine moonstones and guardstones at the foot of the flights of stairs that lead up to the inside of the temple where seated Buddha statues keep a watchful gaze.

Opposite is the ★ **Hatadage Temple F**, where once the sacred tooth of the Buddha was kept. Before then the relic's place of honour was in the ★ **Atadage G**, originally a two-storey building.

Behind the Hatadage you will catch sight of the ★ **Satmahal Prasada H**, a pyramid-shaped, Cambodian-style tower with seven storeys.

NORTH OF THE CITY WALL

Rankoth Vihara I and ★★ **Kiri Vihara J** (12th century) are easily visible from afar. The former was once the largest *dagoba* in Polonnaruwa, the latter the best preserved of the relic shrines that have not been restored.

The impressive walls of the ★★★ **Lankatilaka Image House K**, adorned with huge half-columns and Hindu frescoes, soar to a height of 17m (55ft). The cathedral-like brick structure is the most impressive ruin in the second royal city. Examine closely the carefully worked guardstones and the murals from the 12th century. Unfortunately, the 13-m (40-ft) high standing Buddha in the interior is still headless.

The highlight of Buddhist art in Sri Lanka is undoubtedly ★★★ **Gal Vihara L**, a rock shrine with four Buddha statues.

By the entrance is the largest figure, a 14-m (46-ft) long reclining Buddha in a state of *nirvana*. The upright figure to the left (7m/23ft high) shows the Buddha shortly after his enlightenment. Note the unusual way in which the arms are crossed. Some researchers wonder whether this really is a figure of the Buddha. The two other statues represent the Buddha in a meditative pose.

As with many of the world's most famous sites, it is possible to appreciate the atmosphere of peace and tranquillity only if you are fortunate enough to arrive during one of those rare intervals between two tour parties.

If you have the time and the energy, head a little further north to the small but beautiful **Lotus Pond** Ⓜ and the **Tivanka Image House (Jetavana)** Ⓝ, which contains some interesting murals and friezes.

SOUTH OF THE CITY WALL

Another **rock sculpture** Ⓞ some way to the south is something of a mystery. This extraordinary figure with a beard, exposed upper body and an ox yoke in his hand could be King Parakramabahu or, more likely, a Saivite *rishi* (sage) called Agastaya. Next to him lies the circular ruin of the **Potgul Vihara** Ⓟ, a huge brick structure with four *dagobas*, which was possibly a library.

Map on page 48

Star Attractions
- **Vatadage Temple**
- **Kiri Vihara**
- **Lankatilaka Image House**
- **Gal Vihara**

Hindu Antecedents
Polonnaruwa became the capital of Sri Lanka after the Chola king Rajaraja's annexation of the island in *circa* 1000. Its strategic position overlooking the crossing of the Mahaweli River made it an obvious location. Although the Cholas were defeated in 1073 by Vijayabahu I, they left a legacy of architecture which blended South Indian Hindu forms with local Buddhist traditions.

Potgul Vihara

Map
on page
42

THE LION ROCK

★★★ **Sigiriya** (427km/265 miles), a huge rock rising up out of the plain, is visible from many miles away. Don't be scared off by its dimensions. It only takes about two hours to climb up and down. The effort is repaid by the view from the summit (200m/650ft) over jungle, paddy fields, ponds and distant mountain ranges. It is now about 1,500 years since the murderous Kasyapa escaped to this inaccessible rock to avoid his vengeful brother and built a palace here.

Halfway up the rock is a platform containing the famous Sigiriya murals. Painted many hundreds of years ago on to what is known as the Mirror Wall and coated with a mixture of honey and egg to give a gloss finish, some of the original 500 paintings of women remain; wearing elaborate headwear and jewellery and coloured in green and red tones, they appear to be rising out of clouds.

Take a break at the middle plateau – where soft drinks are available at extortionate prices – before passing the two huge, brick lion paws and setting off up the steep metal staircase. Little has survived on the summit plateau apart from a few walls, steps and a cistern. But it is only from up above that the extent of the ponds, geometrically laid-out gardens and circular paths at the foot of the rock can be fully appreciated.

Below: tourists on elephant-back
Bottom: Sigiriya mural

ANCIENT IRRIGATION

Thousands of workers laboured day in day out for 12 long years, shifting hard, dry soil. The result was the **Parakrama Samudra**, a huge lake formed from three smaller lakes dotted around Polonnaruwa. With an area of 23 sq km (8 sq miles), it is the largest of the 163 tanks that King Parakramabahu built 800 years ago. He was mainly responsible for developing the Sri Lankan irrigation system, which helped farmers to overcome the long dry period.

As well as creating so many reservoirs, he also drained marshland and built canals. To his people he declared: 'Not a single drop of rain shall reach the ocean before man has made use of it.'

But the technology is actually much older. Over 2,000 years ago, Basawak Kulam and Tissa Wewa were built in Anuradhapura. Up to 30,000 *wewas*, linked by countless canals, were created in the Dry Zone and these formed the basis for an agricultural system that would yield two rice crops a year. With the withdrawal of the Sinhalese kings to the south and the abandonment of Polonnaruwa, these man-made constructions fell into disrepair. In the first half of the 20th century only about 7,000 *wewas* remained in working order.

When work began on the Mahaweli Dam project during the 1970s, the engineers applied some of the technology developed by their forebears. This massive project involves the construction of huge dams, reservoirs and hydro-electric power stations to supply land in the Dry Zone with water and Sri Lankan households with electricity.

DAMBULLA CAVE TEMPLES

The five cave temples at ★★★ **Dambulla** (450km/280 miles) rank among the most popular attractions in Sri Lanka, a fact borne out by the number of beggars, souvenir shops and street traders who gather at this sacred spot. Don't shell out the requested Rs 100 for leaving your shoes at the temple entrance, the more usual sum for this service is Rs 10. Tourists themselves are to blame

Star Attractions
● Sigiriya
● Dambulla

Water Storage
The solution to conserving rainwater was arrived at in the 3rd century BC. A 'valve pit', or *bisokotuwa* (much like a modern sluice-gate), meant that large reservoirs could be built which could feed a widespread network of canals. The canals stretched for up to 80km (50 miles), dropping less than 20cm per km (1 foot per mile). A testimony to the skill of these early engineers.

Sigiriya rock at sunset

Map
on page
42

for the photography ban. When a visitor sat on the lap of a Buddha statue, the authorities decided to put a stop to such inappropriate conduct.

Before you set foot in the sacred caves, you must first climb the 122-m (400-ft) rock face in the company of countless – and sometimes rather cheeky – monkeys.

Below: saffron-clad monk
Bottom: giant Buddha
at Dambulla

BUDDHIST IMAGES, HINDU DEITIES

The five caves were first used 2,200 years ago as refuges for monks. The Buddha statues, frescoes and murals, however, probably date from around 1,000 AD. Several of the works of art here have now been restored with the help of UNESCO funds.

The first cave is home to a 14-m (46-ft) long Buddha just before he achieved *nirvana*, with his pupil, Ananda, at his feet. Next comes the largest and finest cave. Here you can admire some 60 Buddha statues, several Hindu deities, two kings and 1,500 Buddha images on the ceiling. At the entrance a drawing shows the Buddha on his way to enlightenment, fighting against the demons of temptation. A bowl in the middle of the 7-m (22-ft) high cave catches holy water dripping from the ceiling.

Three more caves are decorated with statues made from marble, sandalwood and ebony.

HEADING SOUTH

In an enchanting setting by a lake from which bare tree trunks tower up stands **Nalanda Gedige**. First you must cross an embankment to reach this Buddhist image house, which probably dates from the 8th century. It was only recently moved to this spot in order to make way for the Mahaweli Dam scheme.

In many respects the temple is a remarkable piece of art history, one of the rare examples of the fusion of Buddhism and Hinduism. It is the only Buddhist building in the southern Indian Pallava architectural style. Some of the frescoes show erotic scenes.

ANCIENT LIBRARY

★★ **Aluvihara** (489km/303 miles) is a third-century BC rock monastery. It is an important sanctuary for Buddhists, but sees few tourists. Largely undisturbed, the monks produce palm leaf manuscripts, a tradition which goes back about 2,000 years to when the Fourth Buddhist Council made the decision to write down the oral teachings of the Buddha on palm leaves.

One of the guides will demonstrate the process on a strip of palm leaf. The technique has changed over the centuries. Instead of smoothing out the palm leaves in the traditional, time-consuming way, the monks now use an iron. A museum and some rock caves form part of the monastery. Unusually for a sacred site there is a torture rack and murals depicting scenes of torture.

THE ROAD TO KANDY

On the main street in **Matale** you will pass a Hindu temple, the **Sri Muthumariamman Thevasthanam**. Inside, a number of imaginative statues of Hindu gods accept the gifts of the faithful (*puja* times are 8.30am and 4.30pm).

Beside the main road on the final stretch of road (26km/16 miles) to **Kandy** (*see page 35*) are a number of **spice gardens** (*see page 96*) and several **batik shops**.

Star Attraction
● Aluvihara

Craft Villages
Between Kandy and Matale are a number of villages that specialise in handicrafts. At **Palle Hapuvida** you can watch workers applying lacquer to wood and in **Kalapuraya Craftperson's Village** there is a community of metalworkers and woodcarvers. **Gunepana** and **Amunugama** have schools that train performers of traditional dance and drumming.

Bird batik, Aluvihara

Map on page 42

4: Central Highlands

Kandy – Nuwara Eliya – Horton Plains – Adam's Peak – Ella – Badulla (300km/186 miles)

> **British Hill Station**
> The British discovered the site of Nuwara Eliya in 1818, when it was chanced upon by a hunting party. The town itself was founded in 1828, when the governor, Sir Edward Barnes, turned the highland site into a health resort and sanitorium for British officials, after which it soon became a fashionable retreat during the hot season.

Long hikes in Sri Lanka's tropical heat may not initially have much appeal, but in truth the activity poses few problems once you head into the island's mountainous interior. During the 19th century the English withdrew to the Central Highlands in search of relaxation amid the vast tea plantations and rice terraces, the forests in the mist and the bizarre mountain ranges. Nuwara Eliya, for example, a town 'in the clouds', has a mild climate and a colonial feel.

This part of Sri Lanka is a paradise for nature lovers. You can climb the highest and most sacred mountain peaks, but also within reach as day trips are waterfalls, deep gorges and the magnificent views from the Sri Lankan version of the 'end of the world'.

Walking up the track to Nuwara Eliya

UP COUNTRY

The A5 runs to Pusselawa from Kandy via Peradeniya and Gampola. A road then branches off towards Talawakele negotiating mountain passes, running alongside steep precipices and reaching an altitude of 2,100m (6,900ft). At one vantage point the road overlooks two of the finest waterfalls in Sri Lanka. **St Clair Falls** plunges 73m (240ft), **Devon Falls** 86m (282ft).

Some sections of the panoramic route wind alongside the railway track – used by many Sri Lankans as a footpath – following sharp bends beside deep valleys, from where giant trees tower skywards. Hairpin bends snake through the mountain landscape, a delightful mix of rice terraces and tea plantations, palm trees and bamboos, banana trees and eucalyptus woods.

The mild climate allows vegetables more commonly associated with temperate regions, like cabbages and potatoes, to thrive. Vegetation, clinging to the slopes like a lush green carpet, contrasts only with the brightly coloured saris of the tea pluckers. Every day, the female labourers, overwhelmingly Tamil, harvest up to 16kg (36lb) of leaves carried in baskets strapped to their backs. They pick only the young shoots and the bud, earning barely £1/US$1.45 a day for their labours.

Names such as Somerset, Glenford and Edinburgh testify to the British origins of the tea plantations. Tea continues to play a vital role in Sri Lanka's economy and many of the 'factories' along this route are open to visitors.

NUWARA ELIYA

After a tortuous 3-hour drive (A7 via Nanu Oya) ★★ **Nuwara Eliya** finally comes into view – or perhaps not. At an altitude of 1,890m (6,200ft), the weather can be changeable and the hills are often shrouded in mist. Nuwara Eliya (pronounced *Noo-ray-lee-ya*) was the summer hill station for the British colonial masters. It can be wet and cold in these parts so the European settlers would feel at home. When the clouds descend, then the man-made **Gregory Lake** or the summit of **Pidurutalagala**, which rises to 2,524m (8,280ft) behind the town, disappear from view. Many of the villas built in English country-style with gable roofs and towers have open hearths.

The season in 'Sri Lankan Switzerland' lasts from March to May. During these months there is less rain, the flowers in the neatly tended

Star Attraction
● Nuwara Eliya

Below: temperate vegetables
Bottom: Gregory Lake

Map on page 42

The Hill Club
Temporary membership of the Hill Club is available to visitors who wish to stay overnight after having dinner. Contact: The Secretary, The Hill Club, Nuwara Eliya, tel: 052 22653.

Below: giant ferns
Bottom: lake, Horton Plains

gardens blossom, ponies are paraded up and down the racecourse and, of course, hotel prices go sky-high. One experience not to miss is a dinner in the Hill Club *(see page 98)* where hunting trophies adorn the walls. Ties must be worn from 7pm (available for hire). The town's 18-hole golf course is one of the finest in Asia *(see page 103)*.

To the south of Nuwara Eliya are the **Hakgala Botanical Gardens**, lying at the foot of the prominent **Hakgala peak**. Originally these were established as a plantation to grow cinchona for quinine extraction, nowadays they are known for their beautiful array of flowers and the lovely view. Beside the gardens is the **Hakgala Nature Reserve**, home to bear monkeys, sambar and many varieties of birds.

WORLD'S END

★ **Horton Plains** and **World's End** are situated 29km (18 miles) south of Nuwara Eliya. They are best viewed at sunrise as the mists are less likely to spoil the view at that time of day. The road journey and the 2-to-3-hour walk passes through heathland with giant ferns, terraced vegetable gardens and tropical, mist-shrouded forest, where tree branches poke skywards like gnarled fingers.

You reach Big World's End after a 5-km (3-mile) walk from the entrance at Farr Inn. The view from the sheer 1,000-m (3,300-ft) drop is awesome. With luck there will be no mist to impede the panorama over the plains.

You can return along the same path or take a short detour via **Baker's Falls**. At weekends and on public holidays, the isolated World's End site becomes the destination for what seems like a nation migrating.

Horton Plains can be reached from your hotel in Nuwara Eliya in about 1½ hours by jeep. The road there is very bumpy. It is well worth making the effort to reach the 'end of the world', though there is an admission charge. What is called Poor Man's World's End, reached by heading east along a track from Anderson Lodge, is a free alternative.

ADAM'S PEAK

Thankfully there is still no entrance charge at
★ ★★ **Adam's Peak** (Sri Pada), Sri Lanka's
sacred mountain, set in the heart of the spectacular **Peak Wilderness** nature reserve and bird
paradise. If you have made up your mind to climb
Sri Pada, after 9,600 steps you may well not want
to see another flight of steps for days, but this
excursion will prove to be an unforgettable
encounter with the country and its people – a very
special sort of summit meeting.

A good starting point is Brown's Upper Glencairn Bungalow in Dickoya. Aim to set out from
here at about 1am so that you can begin the climb
up the steps in Dalhousie at the foot of the peak
at 2 or 3am. If you get a move on, then you can
complete the climb in 2 to 3 hours.

At the top it will be cold and windy, and warm
clothing and sturdy footwear are advisable. The
pilgrimage season begins on the *poya* day in
December, continuing until April, and the summit route gets congested during those months.
Between May and October the peak is often
obscured by cloud. Return along the same route.
The Ratnapura-side descent (see page 61) is not
recommended.

The dense forests of the ★★ **Peak Wilderness
Sanctuary** stretch for some 40km (24 miles) to
the west of Sri Pada.

Star Attractions
● Adam's Peak
● Peak Wilderness Sanctuary

Below: Peak Wilderness
Bottom: panning for jewels

Map on page 42

Birds and Gardens

Between Bandarawela and Welimada is the small village of Mirahawatte. This is home to the **Uva Herbarium**, a garden dedicated to growing herbs and re-establishing forests. Not only is this a lovely place for a picnic, but it is also excellent for spotting and photographing many species of birds.

Buduruwagala, main Buddha

ON BY TRAIN

The best way to continue onward from Nuwara Eliya is by catching a train at **Nanu Oya**. From the panorama carriage on the afternoon train, you can lean back in a comfortable armchair and enjoy a stirring natural spectacle: when it starts to get dark, the outlines of the mountains stand out on the horizon like burning flames.

The journey continues through the sleepy little town of **Haputale**, once the haunt of the tea millionaire Thomas Lipton. Here is also the Addisham Benedictine monastery, modelled on Leeds Castle in Kent, England. Further on is the the lively junction and mountain spa resort of **Bandarawela** (1,230m/4,035ft). This is where some of the best tea in Sri Lanka is produced. The former tea planters' club is now a comfortable hotel.

Further still, the little town of **Ella** is an ideal place for travellers in need of a rest to stop off. Attractions waiting to be discovered close by include the Ella Gorge with some fine views, the Rawana Ella Falls, which drops a height of 8m (26ft) and, situated in a delightful spot by a stream, the Dowa Rock Temple. Associated with the epic *Ramayana*, Ella is held to be the place where King Ravanna of Lanka held Sita, the wife of Lord Rama captive.

IMPRESSIVE FALLS

If you are touring by car, then you should include in your itinerary the ★ **Diyaluma Falls** where, by a bend in the road beyond Wellawaya, water crashes down a 171-m (561-ft) precipice. These are very spectacular when swollen by monsoon rains. Also try to fit in a visit to the carvings of ★ **Buduruwagala**. These seven figures with a 16-m (52-ft) high Lord Buddha in the centre are said to have been hacked out of the black granite rock 1,000 years ago.

The end of this route and the mountain railway line is **Badulla**, a romantic spot surrounded by tea plantations. One worthwhile excursion from Badulla is to **Dunhinda Falls**, where a fountain of misty haze tumbles 58m (190ft).

5: South of Colombo

Colombo – Ratnapura (– Nuwara Eliya) – Sinharaja Forest – Bulutota Pass – South coast (270km/167 miles)

Map
on page
60

Overlooking Colombo and the coast are hillsides that conceal a valuable buried treasure. In Ratnapura – the 'city of gems' – you can look over the shoulders of craftsmen as they demonstrate how to turn a mud-smeared chunk of stone into a thing of beauty. From Ratnapura winding roads lead either up into the cool hill country or down to the south coast.

Below: collecting rubber
Bottom: rubber plantation

As you descend towards the sea, you can experience the strange sights and sounds of Sri Lanka's last jungle. It is quite possible to cover this section in one day, but it would be better and more enjoyable to take your time and spread the journey out over two or three days.

COLLECTING RUBBER

Rubber plantations line the road from Colombo to Ratnapura (101km/63 miles). Rubber trees thrive at these mid-range altitudes. Every day about a quarter of a litre (just under ½ pint) of the milky resin drips into a small bowl from a cut in the tree trunk. At the rubber factory the latex is treated with chemical additives and thickened,

Map below

pressed into slabs and then hung up to dry – the smell is foul, not unlike curdled milk. The raw material is exported cheaply all over the world in exchange for dollars, re-appearing as shoe soles, car tyres and condoms.

The trade in gems is far more lucrative, although not for the miners themselves. Some of the mines are scattered around in the rice fields, not just around Ratnapura. The gem-bearing strata are excavated using a centuries-old techniques, the miners risking their lives in underground shafts and tunnels for a few rupees.

Children in Ratnapura

CITY OF GEMS

Life in ★★ **Ratnapura** revolves around jewellery, workshops, exhibitions and auctions, with mainly Muslims clad in white calling the tune. On virtually every street corner shadowy figures are on the look-out for gullible buyers, preferably tourists. In the workshops, craftsmen produce by hand something that will later sparkle

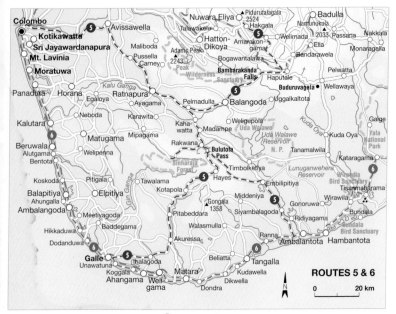

ROUTES 5 & 6

0   20 km

seductively in a glass display cabinet. The grinding wheel is foot-operated and the gold for the frames is smelted over glowing embers.

Ratnapura National Museum houses a model of a gem pit, plus a display of prehistoric fossils found in the search for the precious stones and a jewellery exhibition (closed Friday). One particularly valuable collection is displayed in the **★★ Gem Museum** (6 Ehelepola Mawatha). Not only can visitors see a demonstration of jewel polishing, but the finished product is also sold at fixed prices and visitors are guaranteed that the stones are genuine and of good quality.

Adam's Peak, or Sri Pada, is usually visible from Ratnapura. It may not look far away, but think twice before approaching it from this side. The climb involves a 15–25km (9–16 mile) march through spectacular countryside. While there is no question that it can be done, the trek does involve following unmarked, unlit paths beside steep precipices. Unless you are a seasoned hiker who enjoys a challenge, take the route from Kandy or Nuwara Eliya (*see page 57*).

INTO THE HILLS

From Ratnapura you can climb up to Nuwara Eliya over rapidly rising hill country past the Kirindi Ella waterfall and the caves near Balangoda.

Before reaching Haputale take a turning to the **Bambarakanda Falls**. With a drop of 241m (791ft), this waterfall is the highest on the island. After the rainy season, huge volumes of water plunge downwards.

The road snakes its way so steeply upwards that the altitude starts to affect the ears and it can also get a little chilly. Travellers are greeted by the aroma of the pine forest and a fine view over the terraced vegetable plots. White mosques, *dagobas* and Hindu *kovils* shine out from the green and undulating landscape. You will initially find the sight of Sri Lankans wearing fur hats and balaclavas rather strange. Round every corner is a stall with a colourful array of fruit, vegetables and flowers, until the road reaches **Nuwara Eliya** (*see page 55*) at an altitude of 1,890m (6,200ft).

Star Attractions
● **Ratnapura**
● **Gem Museum**

Sacred Peak
Sri Pada, or Adam's Peak, was regarded as sacred long before the arrival of either Hinduism or Buddhism on Sri Lanka. The indigenous Vedda people call the mountain Samanala Kanda – Saman is one of the Veddah's four presiding deities.

Below: in the Gem Museum
Bottom: tropical fruit

Map on page 60

Wildlife Contacts
Visits to Sri Lanka's sanctuaries and wildlife parks must be booked through the Department of Wildlife Conservation. They can be contacted at: 493 T.B. Jaya Mawatha, Colombo 10, tel: 691 321/688 261–2.

HEADING SOUTH

If you prefer to head south from Ratnapura towards the coast, then be prepared for a hike through the ★★★ **Sinharaja Forest**, the last tropical rainforest in Sri Lanka. Waterproof clothing is essential. Not a ray of sunlight penetrates the dense tree canopy on which the rain patters. Insects hum and chirp incessantly, but only the butterflies display any colour in this evergreen world. Primeval giants tower majestically upwards as if seeking an escape route from man's clutches. Environmental protection groups saved this paradise from felling by a timber factory and the forest has been a nature reserve now since 1989.

The best time to visit is between February and April, when it usually only rains in the afternoon. A tour can be booked from your hotel in Ratnapura as a day excursion with jeep and driver. You need to be away from there before sunrise so that you arrive at the reserve about 8am. The hike along the 5-km (3-mile) track with guide normally takes about 3 hours. If you wish to spend the night in the hostel, then you must obtain permission from the Department of Wildlife Conservation *(see adjacent panel)*.

Nearby is the **Uda Walawe National Park**, covering some 308 sq km (119 sq miles), home to around 600 elephants. In the middle of the park is the **Uda-Walawe reservoir**, where with a little bit of luck you will be able to observe a herd of elephants bathing (admission charge). The park is also home to a wide variety of deer, wild boar and jackals.

INTO THE LOW COUNTRY

Continue your journey towards the coast to the **Bulutota Pass** where the road squeezes out from the Sabaragamuwa hills at 1,500m (4,921ft) and then descends to the coastal province, affording spectacular views over the plains. The winding road forks after Akuressa, heading east to Galle and west to Matara, both of which are on the coast *(see Route 6)*.

Sinharaja rainforest

6: Coastal Attractions

Colombo – Kalutara – Beruwala – Bentota – Ambalangoda – Hikkaduwa – Galle – Matara – Hambantota – Tissamaharama – Yala National Park – Kataragama (283km/175 miles)

For the next few days you will be following palm-lined, sandy beaches with a cool sea breeze on your back. There are plenty of opportunities for watersports, boat trips and tours into the hinterland and beyond. You can watch the famous mask-carvers at work in the studios of Ambalangoda, and the stilt fishermen near Weligama. And do try to get up early to watch proceedings at the fish markets. Colonial history comes alive in the fort at Galle, while Yala National Park is the place for an elephant safari by jeep.

COLOMBO'S SOUTHERN BEACHES

Galle Road, the long coast road, soon reaches **Mount Lavinia**. This suburb of Colombo has for a long time been one of the smarter bathing beaches and the ★★ **Mount Lavinia Hotel** was a meeting place for the world's rich and famous for many years. Built in 1806 in the style of an Italian palace, it was formerly the seat of the British Governor, Edward Barnes. He was forced to sell the house by the government in London

Map on page 60

Star Attractions
- Sinharaja Forest
- Mount Lavinia Hotel

Below: fisherman mending nets, Hikkaduwa
Bottom: masks for sale

Map on page 60

Below: Gangatilaka Vihara
Bottom: bridge over
the Kalu Ganga

who disapproved of his extravagant lifestyle. It became a hotel in 1877. When the sun is setting over the sea, the spacious terrace which looks across towards Colombo 10km (7 miles) to the north is a wonderful place to relax. Unfortunately, the architects who designed the new wing of the hotel completely ignored the original building's Italian features and desecrated the dignified facade with a six-storey concrete block.

Away from the Mount Lavinia Hotel, the resort has lost its exclusive cachet – apart from the prices. Beach life is spoilt by its proximity to the capital and women on their own can expect to be pestered – and not just in the evening.

THE KALU GANGA

Towering above the lush green banks of the Kalu Ganga is the ★ **Gangatilaka Vihara** of **Kalutara** – the gleaming white symbol of a small town, where rubber and the best mangosteens on the island are traded. Visitors to the temple will find a calm and peaceful atmosphere with the sweet aroma of burning incense sticks permeating the air. Buddhists place lotus blossom on the altar and sink into a deep meditative state.

In the middle of the large domed hall stands the *dagoba* with the walled-off reliquary shrine. Colourful pictures on the inside of the dome depict events from the life of the Buddha and repay close observation. The view from above sweeps across the mouth of the Kalu Ganga to the wide turquoise blue ocean and along the seemingly endless line of palm trees beside the coast.

A cruise on the Kalu Ganga makes a good alternative to sunbathing by the pool. The boat glides past apparently untouched banks, where monitor lizards lurk camouflaged by the mangrove thicket; black cormorants sit proudly in the treetops with their wings stretched out to dry. Little is seen of the tiny riverside settlements apart from an occasional church tower and a plume of smoke. Sometimes the sound of a cock crowing or monks chanting breaks the silence. Villagers, often lathered up to their ears, appear by the banks to wash. Sometimes men appear carrying empty baskets which they fill with sand dug from the river bed – it is then used as a building material.

Star Attraction
● Brief Gardens

BEACH RESORTS

It is said that Arabs were the first settlers in **Beruwala** about 1,000 years ago. The oldest surviving mosque in Sri Lanka, the **Kachchimalai**, was probably built about 500 years ago. As the population still consists of many Muslims, a festival is staged here every year to mark the end of Ramadan. There is a fine view over the harbour – usually full of colourful fishing boats – from the hill. As the sun rises fishermen sell the previous night's catch at the fish market.

The long string of hotels beside the fine beach has been very popular with German tourists for many years and street traders here are likely to address Western visitors initially in German. Clustered around the Beruwala-Moragalla tourist complex are countless stalls selling sun hats, necklaces, shells, T-shirts and batiks.

Tourist hotels overlook the long, wide sandy beach to beyond Bentota. Alutgama and Bentota lie on opposite banks of the Bentota Ganga (bridge and ferry available). ★ **Bentota** has been appearing in the holiday catalogues for many

★★ Brief Gardens
16km (10 miles) inland between Beruwala and Bentota are the gardens of Brief. These were created by the landscape artist and sculptor Bevis Bawa (brother to Sri Lanka's most famous architect). Work started on the gardens in 1920 and continued up until Bawa's death in 1992. Brief was left to the manager, Dooland da Silva, who is happy to show visitors around. For an appointment ring him on: 034 70462.

Beruwala

Map on page 60

years and has not always had a good press, but it is in fact better than its reputation. Situated in a stunning position between river and sea, the broad, palm-lined beach of fine sand is seldom overcrowded.

LOCAL LIFE

The three resorts of Beruwala, Alutgama and Bentota all offer fitness facilities and every imaginable watersports activity.

Along the coast road you will see many large signs advertising **hatcheries**. However, most of these businesses where turtles are bred are more concerned with profit than nurturing these endangered species *(see page 13)*. On the beach local boat-owners offer cruises around the Bentota lagoon, often including a visit to the Buddhist Galapatha temple.

If you follow a footpath starting a few hundred metres south of the bridge (on the Bentota side), you will be rewarded with a fascinating insight into Sri Lankan life. Just a short distance from the coast – still close to the air-conditioned hotels, the whirlpools, the discos, the exotic cocktails and all the other tourist trappings – rural life continues its traditional course much as it has done for centuries.

In the plantations, coconuts are hacked down

Below: conservation notice
Bottom: hawksbill turtle

from palm trees with a machete and oil is squeezed from the dried coconut flesh *(copra)* with the aid of an ox-driven mill. Wrinkled old men wearing sarongs sit in front of their houses, discussing reports in the *Daily News*. Now and then, water buffalo obstinately block the way, while women kneel by the river bank slapping their washing forcibly against a rock. Meanwhile children, ever hopeful for a sweet, follow tourists around.

TRADITIONAL CRAFTS

Ahungalla has slowly become a draw for holi-daymakers from all over the world, thanks mainly to one of the finest beaches in the world. The 5-star Triton Hotel is the main focal point. Along the coast road cows graze between the grave-stones in the cemeteries, a boy sits on a stone and waves at the passing holidaymakers, while on the other side of the road ocean waves crash on to the beach and palm trees wave in the wind.

The next stop **Ambalangoda**, the mask carv-ing and puppeteer centre *(see page 64)*, is a lively market town with a station and a number of craft shops. Do stop here and pay a visit to the ★★ **Mask Museum**. Several of the rooms are devoted to the history and significance of this tra-ditional craft (Ariyapala & Sons, 426 Pata-bendimulla, tel: 09 273 73).

If you are interested in the mining of moon-stones – a type of gemstone, and not the moonstones seen on temple floors – then you can learn something of what is involved in the **Mitiyagoda** mine situated nearby. About one third of the rough stones are suitable for processing into gems and this work is carried out in the small workshop next door.

TOURIST TRAP

The image of **Hikkaduwa** has changed. Once a hippy rendezvous with a bad reputation, it is now a mecca for package holiday tourists. The 3-km (2-mile) long resort consists mainly of boutiques, batik shops and wooden huts selling leather

Star Attraction
● Mask Museum

Environmental Damage
The much vaunted coral reef, at least by local guides, at Hikkaduwa is now com-pletely dead. This is due to very insen-sitive tourist development (eg. damage from boat propellors taking people out to see the reef) and from pollution, primarily raw sewage from the resort and petrol from the boats. Don't fall for any tours offering a trip to the reef.

Below: Mask Museum
Bottom: Hikkaduwa beach

Map
on page
60

Maritime Museum
If you have time, take a look around this museum (open daily, 9am–5pm). It has exhibits dealing with all aspects of life in and around the sea, including a 'walk-in' diorama showing the construction of coral reefs.

Below: the Dutch East India Company crest
Bottom: Galle Fort lighthouse

goods, jewellery and woodcarvings. It is impossible to say how many guesthouses and hotels, pizza restaurants, garden eateries and bars line the main street, but clearly Hikkaduwa is a good place to buy your souvenirs or to buy tailor-made clothing. Prices are, of course, set at tourist levels and haggling is the norm. Power cuts sometimes interrupt shopping during the evening. Traditional dance shows are held in most hotels. Gathered on the beach are traders, contortionists and fortune-tellers, perhaps even one of the last remaining hippy gurus with straggly dreadlocks. The best place to swim is in the south, from Narigama, where you cannot hurt yourself on the coral reefs.

GALLE

In 1987 UNESCO declared **Galle**, a town close to the southern tip of the island known for its narrow alleyways, crooked houses with verandas, small inner courtyards, ornate lanterns and unpronounceable street names, a World Heritage Site. Although the town's Dutch past is very much in evidence, Arab influences have had more impact on the lives of the inhabitants. Arab settlers first arrived here 1,000 years ago, leaving their cultural trademark of mosques, white robes and caps.

The fort was built by the Portuguese at the end of the 16th century and later extended by the Dutch. It is the best-preserved fortified site in Sri Lanka. An evening stroll around the ★★★ **fortress walls** is something of a tradition among the locals and tourists alike. Every visitor's photo album is bound to have a shot of the **lighthouse** and the splendid **Meera Mosque**. The scrolled gables of the **Groote Kerk** reveal the Dutch origins of the 200-year-old church.

The neighbouring **New Oriental Hotel** dates from 1684. It has been a hotel since 1863 and still exudes a quaint Victorian charm.

The small **Historical Mansion** museum (daily 9am–6pm) in Leyn Baan Street has a collection of traditional Galle handicrafts, such as ebony carvings and lacework.

Away from the historic town centre, it is worth

exploring the busy **fish market** and the covered **bazaar**. But do be careful of the many touts who use a variety of ploys to lure the gullible into the nearest jeweller's shop.

The **Southern Gem Museum** in the west of the town has a small collection of jewellery, carvings and antiques (Colombo Street; daily 9am–5pm).

Star Attractions
- Galle Fortress Walls
- Unawatuna

UNAWATUNA BEACH

Not long ago only a few visitors knew of ★★ **Unawatuna**'s wide, curving bay with a picture-book sweep of golden beach overlooked by rocky hills and palm trees. Even during the monsoon period, you can splash around in the shallow waters. Bobbing up and down on the water are fishing boats, whose owners offer trips to the offshore coral reefs. Competent swimmers can make their own way there – it is not as far as the fishermen would like you to think.

But as in all those special places known only to a few, wooden huts quickly started to appear calling themselves 'restaurant' or 'guesthouse'. Then came problems with the water supply. There is no sewage system and so waste passes straight into the sea. In many of the hotels near the beach, the water that emerges from the shower-head is an orangy-brown colour. The piles of rubbish that accumulate on the beach are cleared away for the

Below: collecting coral
Bottom: Unawatuna beach

Map
on page
60

holiday season, but the Ministry of Tourism has recently ordered the demolition of some of the guesthouses and new resort hotels should give the town a rather smarter look.

THE SOUTH COAST

The inhabitants of the villages along the south coast road must be hoping that they will be spared Unawatuna-style development. There is a series of small fishing villages around the southern tip of the island extending as far as Hambantota, many with idyllic bays where over recent years a number of hotel and chalet complexes have been built: Koggala, Ahangama, Weligama, Mirissa and Tangalla. Strong underwater currents are a hazard in some places, such as Mirissa.

Below: fishing boat, Weligama
Bottom: stilt fisherman

Koggala is well known for its potters who pile brightly coloured clay jugs by the roadside to sell to passing travellers. Behind the town lies the extensive Koggala Lake, where during World War II British hydroplanes landed. Now local fishermen will row holidaymakers around the palm-lined lake for a few hours – stopping off now and then for tea breaks with families who run spice gardens.

On the way to Weligama you may well see the fishermen who perch for hours on stilts out in the bay above the surf. This traditional way of

fishing requires strength and endurance as the men must keep their balance on the poles. These **stilt fishermen** usually work at dawn or dusk, but it is rumoured that the men mount their stilts when they see a bus full of tourists pull up.

In **Weligama** itself monitor lizards lie in wait near the market to feed off fish scraps. Holiday-makers are warmly welcomed in some of the nearby factories and studios, e.g. the lace work-shops, the snake farm (Telijjawila), and the rub-ber and batik workshops and coconut factories, where the 'tree of life' *(see page 14)* is processed.

In the bay, on **Count de Maunay's Island**, is a beautiful 1930s villa built by a French count and still in private hands – so don't try to land.

> **The Leper King**
> In a small park just west of the centre of Weligama is a 3-metre (12-ft) high carving of the legendary character, Kustaraja ('leper king'). He is said to have arrived in Sri Lanka stricken with lep-rosy and to have been cured by drink-ing nothing but coconut water for three months.

FISH MARKETS

It is worth getting up in the morning to witness the colourful scenes that are enacted at the coastal fish markets. Beside the often sheltered harbours, such as at **Mirissa** and **Tangalla**, clusters of men surround the shiny sea harvest, examining it closely, before haggling noisily over ray, shark and smaller fish. A metre-long tuna is loaded onto the bike and transported home.

Be prepared to see dead dolphins among the catch. They sometimes get caught up in the nets – possibly on purpose – but rather than waste the meat the fishermen sell the protected mammals to restaurants and to villagers from the interior.

Fish market, Negombo

MATARA

The southbound railway line ends in the busy town of ★★ **Matara**. There are two Dutch forts either side of the Nilwala Ganga. The Star Fort is the more interesting of the two. This dates from 1763 and now houses a small museum. If you want to learn how batik designs are produced, then do pay a visit to **Jez-Look Batiks** *(see page 99)*. On the other side of the river, Matara Fort contains much of the old town and is quiet and peaceful. Many of the best guesthouses are found here

Two huge, modern Buddha statues have been

Map on page 60

Mulgirigalla

Heading inland from Wewurukannala brings you to the Pahala Vihara Cave Temple at Mulgirigalla. The spectacular rock rises 105m (350ft) out of the forest and has beautifully painted temples carved into five levels. The site was probably founded in the 1st century BC and important ola-leaf manuscripts found here helped to translate Sri Lanka's most informative ancient text, the *Mahavamsa*.

erected near Matara. In the middle of the ★ **Weherehena Temple** is a 40-m (130-ft) high Buddha in a seated position. On the walls in the underground rooms, the life of the Buddha is depicted in comic-book style.

If this Buddha is not sufficiently impressive for you, then beyond **Dondra**, Sri Lanka's southernmost point, head inland at **Dikwella** to the ★ **Wewurukannala Temple**, part of which dates back to the mid-18th century, where you can see the largest Buddha statue on the island.

Since the end of the 1960s the meditating, 50-m (160-ft) high Buddha has been surveying the surrounding palm groves and rice fields. Again there is a display of comic-strip paintings portraying the life of the Buddha. At both temples, visitors can climb to the top of the statue and peer over the shoulder of the Enlightened One.

Near the fishing village of **Kudawella** there is a natural spectacle that you should include on your itinerary: the ★ **Blow Holes**. High seas, especially during the southwest monsoon in June, force water vertically through a natural rock chimney and then 20m (65ft) into the air. The rougher the seas, the higher the fountain.

THE DRY ZONE

Further east towards **Ambalantota** and **Hambantota** the scenery changes rapidly. This is the Dry Zone. Salt lakes, grassy steppes, dunes and cacti replace the coconut palm groves and banana trees, the characteristic backdrop along the southwest coast. Herds of buffalos cross the road causing the often overloaded buses to brake dangerously.

The royal town of **Tissamaharama** (formerly Mahagama and now usually just called Tissa) lies beside the **Tissa Wewa**, a reservoir that dates from the 3rd century BC. An island in the middle of the lake is home to a rich birdlife. You can walk along the shores of the lake to the 2,000-year-old ruins. Clearly visible are the remains of the royal palace, a lakeside monastery as well as two large *dagobas* in the paddy fields.

Tissamaharama is the ideal starting point for an

Blow Holes' sign

excursion to the Yala National Park or Katar-agama *(see below)*. Some good diving waters lie off the coast of the Yala National Park: the **Great and Little Basses Reef**.

An hour by boat from the beach is a ships' graveyard, but because of the monsoons diving is only safe in March and April.

Birding enthusiasts will appreciate the nature reserves at **Wirawila** and **Bundala**, close to Tissa. The reservoirs are favourite haunts for flamingos and other exotic birds.

Star Attraction
● Yala (Ruhuna)

YALA (RUHUNA)

Excursions into ★★★ **Yala National Park** (also known as Ruhuna; admission charge) are organised by many of the hotels and private operators along the southwest coast. Check that the private tours are for the park itself. Some jeeps simply drive round the outside. The best time to visit is early in the morning soon after sunrise, or else at twilight, but day guests must leave the park before darkness falls. Also available are night-time safaris, when you are most likely to see wild animals (camp-fire party included).

Jungle tours usually include overnight accommodation in tents and food. One company that organises the trips is Hemtours, Sir Ernest de Silva Mawatha, Colombo 7, tel: 01 575 300, fax: 574

Below: sign for Yala National Park
Bottom: flooded rain trees, Tissa Wewa

Map on page 60

Viewing at Yala

Yala's location in the dry zone makes it an ideal place to view Sri Lanka's larger mammals. The dry thorn scrub interspersed with small dusty glades is more akin to the African plains than the jungle found elsewhere in South Asia.

Below: buffalo in paddies
Bottom: puja, Kataragama

560. Accommodation is available (maximum of three days) in the eight bungalows belonging to the National Park but these must be booked in advance in Colombo. Contact the Department of Wildlife Conservation, 493 T.B. Jaya Mawatha, Colombo 10, tel: 01 691 321. The park is closed during the dry season from the end of August to October.

The jeep shoots along the gravel track through the grassy plain, passing waterholes where crocodiles, water buffalo and herons gather. Wild elephants may be spotted grazing in the undergrowth and brambles. Occasionally they walk out on to the track, in which case driver and passengers must stay in the vehicle. At close-quarters the elephants seems tame and tourists are tempted to leave the jeep, but it is in these circumstances that fatalities have occurred.

RELIGIOUS FESTIVALS

Kataragama, 15km (10 miles) north of Tissa, is, along with Adam's Peak, the most important religious pilgrimage site in Sri Lanka. The town is divided by the Menik River, the temple on one bank and the residential area on the other. The presiding deity of the temple is Kataragama Deviyo, also known as Skanda/Murukan, who is represented by his spear, or *vel*. This is kept in the Maha Devala, the most sacred shrine of the complex, where there are daily *pujas* at 4.30am, 10.30am and 6.30pm. Hindus, Buddhists and Muslims all hold the shrine as sacred and worship here

The ★★ **Hindu festival** draws thousands of devotees for a two-week period around the full moon in July and August. As the Kandy Sacred Tooth *perahera* takes place at the same time, pilgrims have to make the choice.

Tourists unsure which to choose should note that the Kandy procession follows a fixed schedule and spectators can watch the parades from a stand. If you enjoy pushing your way through the masses, staying up all night, and the chance to witness the fascinating spectacle of ritual penance and fire-walking, you are likely to prefer Kataragama.

The East Coast

Snow-white beaches, some 100 metres wide, stretch endlessly along Sri Lanka's east coast. On one side runs a belt of green palms, on the other lies crystal-clear ocean as far as the horizon. The finest, most unspoilt of Sri Lanka's beaches lie between Pottuvil and Kuchchaveli.

Clusters of fishing boats betray the fact that this idyllic strip of land is in fact inhabited. Whales and dolphins appreciate the east coast's tranquillity and quite often appear off Trincomalee, while coral reefs close to the shore provide an underwater spectacle for snorkellers. Bathed in unbroken sunshine from March to November, the east coast enjoys a climate that is too good to be true. The tourist industry's plans for expansion envisage resort complexes Bentota-style, plus holiday entertainment, but while the civil war rages, all such projects must remain filed away.

OFF-LIMITS BEACHES

Some 20 years ago backpackers from all over the world headed for the east coast beaches, mainly Nilaveli near Trincomalee, Kalkudah and Arugam Bay. The Australians discovered the latter resort and arrived en masse with their surfboards, thus raising the profile of this beautiful bay. In the early

Map at front

Star Attraction
● **Kataragama festival**

Below: coconut palm
Bottom: East Coast beach

Map at front

Lover's Leap
Also known as Swami Rock, this headland in Trincomalee is where a Dutch official's daughter, Francina van Reede, jumped off after her husband had deserted her. Although her suicide attempt was unsuccessful (she remarried after eight years), her father erected a pillar to mark the incident.

1980s bungalow complexes were built to supplement the basic guesthouses, but the war soon wrecked the hotelier's long-term plans. Supplies could not be guaranteed and travel restrictions limited holiday activities. The tourists left and have not returned.

Then Tamil rebels moved into the holiday homes. Large parts of the Eastern Province came under the control of the LTTE. Many of the closed hotels were plundered and burned down.

TRINCOMALEE

The towns of Trincomalee and Batticaloa are currently under government control, but many Tamil rebels withdrew to the region around Batticaloa, when forced to abandon their headquarters in Jaffna in December 1995. The cat-and-mouse game between rebels and government troops has gone on for more than a decade. If the Tamil Tigers are driven from one corner of the island, they simply regroup in another. The army cannot contain the guerrillas, let alone defeat them.

The only place on the east coast where tourist accommodation is maintained – some guesthouses have even reopened – is **Nilaveli**, near the only largeish town, ★★ **Trincomalee**. In the third-century BC the town was home to the largest Hindu temple in Sri Lanka, but it was destroyed 1,800 years later by the Portuguese.

The new **Tirukonesvaram Kovil** was built on its foundations. Set in a spectacular spot on the Swami Rock, it is one of the largest and most important Hindu temples on the island.

Trincomalee boasts one of the world's finest natural harbours. During the 17th and 18th centuries, it was at the centre of much colonial wrangling. During World War II, it was an allied base and a target for Japanese bombers. The harbour is one of the main stumbling blocks to a peaceful settlement of the Tamil problem. For the Tamils, Trincomalee must be an important component in an autonomous 'Tamil Eelam', but the government is unwilling to abandon what could be a lucrative economic asset.

A Tamil fighter, Jaffna

The eastern side of Sri Lanka is relatively thinly populated as the land is dry and infertile. But the Mahaweli irrigation and dam programme, begun in the 1970s, is bringing life to the parched soil. Sri Lanka's longest river, the Mahaweli Ganga, flows into the Indian Ocean near Trincomalee.

A few decades ago the coastal towns and fishing villages were populated by Tamils and Muslims. Under the Mahaweli scheme, many Sinhalese have been resettled in the east in ethnically mixed villages, but they live in fear of repeated attacks by the LTTE.

Caution Advised

Whether to explore the east coast is a decision which depends primarily on political developments. However, even if the weapons are silenced, then the ever-present military guards, checkpoints and overcrowded refugee camps are unlikely to create the atmosphere for a happy holiday. Getting there will not be easy. Many Sinhalese drivers are afraid to venture east. Rumours of mined roads abound; all flights and train services from Colombo to Trincomalee have been stopped. At present a visit to the east coast would be ill-advised, but if you are determined to go, check out the security situation with your embassy, tour operators and the Ceylon Tourist Board in Colombo.

Star Attraction
● Trincomalee

Below: government recruitment poster
Bottom: refugees at Jaffna railway station

Map at front

The North

Sri Lanka reveals a completely different face in the north. The land is flat, dry and monotonous, with tiny islands, lagoons and salt lakes dotted around the Jaffna peninsula. With the aid of an extensive irrigation and well system, the Tamils have successfully transformed the barren, chalky soil to grow mainly vegetables, and also the best mangoes on the island.

The life of the Tamils is heavily influenced by India, only 35km (22 miles) to the north across the Palk Strait. Cultural ties between the Sri Lankan and South Indian Tamils operate on many levels: the written and spoken language, food, religion, even the agricultural methods derive from southern Indian traditions. Hundreds of Hindu *kovils* and churches – many Tamils are Christians – have been built on the Jaffna peninsula. A distinctive part of the Hindu temple is the southern Indian-style towering entrance *(gopuram)*, which sports countless colourful deities.

JAFFNA

The centre of the north, **Jaffna**, was the second-largest town in Sri Lanka before the start of the civil war. Tamil kings reigned over the kingdom of Nallur from the 13th century until 1619 when the Portuguese and later the Dutch incorporated the peninsula into their colonial empires.

A university was founded in 1974 and Jaffna became the spiritual and cultural capital of the Sri Lankan Tamils. After the country-wide massacre of 1983, many Tamils fled to Jaffna, but since the government's major offensive of 1995 it has become a ghost town. The international aid agencies talk of as many as 500,000 refugees fleeing the peninsula. The heavily censored Sri Lankan newspapers reported that some 2,500 people died in the bombing and fighting, but the number of casualties was in fact much higher.

It was here during the 1970s, in the home of the Indian Tamils, opposition to Sinhalese dominance grew. The call for a separate Tamil state became

The Current Situation

At the time of going to press there appeared to be no end in sight to the conflict.

In 1995 Sri Lankan troops successfully recaptured Jaffna. However, the LTTE reaction to military defeat was to launch a wave of terrorist attacks, mostly bombings aimed at Colombo and Kandy.

The government occupation of Jaffna has been accompanied by as many atrocities on their side as by the Tigers and mass graves have recently been uncovered in Jaffna.

In 2000 the Tigers achieved their biggest victory against the government to date, by taking the strategically important Elephant Pass and pushing forward to the outskirts of Jaffna itself. On Christmas Eve the LTTE called a unilateral ceasefire and asked for dialogue with the government. These overtures were ignored and the government has imposed even greater restrictions on the population of Jaffna while launching what amounts to all-out war.

Such tactics have failed miserably in the past to defeat the Tigers and the added pressure on Sri Lanka's economy points to a miserable future for those caught up in the conflict.

ever louder. Nowhere else in Sri Lanka has suffered as much from the civil war as the north. The state of emergency soon became part of everyday life on the Jaffna peninsula. Repeated military attacks and economic embargoes weakened the region and its infrastructure.

In 1990, after the rebels had taken the peninsula under political control, the region became a *de facto* Tamil state. Guerrilla leader, Prabhakaran, ran the LTTE headquarters from here. The organisation's red, white and gold flag with the tiger head fluttered in the wind alongside posters of the 13-year-old martyrs from the ranks of the notorious 'Tiger Babies', identifiable by the cyanide capsules around their necks.

The LTTE runs a totalitarian regime in the Jaffna peninsula. The rebels demand both the support of all Tamils – and their children – for the war, and also their money. Consequently, the Tigers, founded in 1972, are now a highly disciplined military organisation, which can call on between 5,000 and 10,000 people. Anyone who could afford to escape from the conflict paid 'exit money' (Rs 10,000) to the LTTE and left for the south or emigrated abroad.

From the point of view of the tourist, the north is a definite no-go area. For the time being, nobody would even dare to predict if and when this situation will change.

Below: papaya
Bottom: LTTE memorials

Religion in Sri Lanka

That the various religious groups in Sri Lanka coexist peacefully is clear for all visitors to see. *Dagobas*, Hindu *kovils*, mosques and churches are the architectural expression of a highly religious society. Take a tour of Galle Old Town and the sound of Muslim prayers will resonate from the mosques and prayer rooms. The sound of church bells by the beach at Negombo may not be what you are expecting in a tropical setting. The Christian holy figures and crosses by the roadside may also be a surprise.

THE BUDDHA AS A SHINING EXAMPLE

Gleaming white *dagobas* surrounded by a jungle landscape, outsized Buddha figures, monks with shaven heads in bright orange-coloured robes, the scent of incense sticks in the shops – these are all expressions of a faith that is followed by 70 percent of the population. In every village there is a sacred Bo tree, bedecked with brightly coloured votive flags. Beneath it the people kneel and pay their respects to the Buddha, requesting the fulfilment of their wishes. At the entrance to a temple, the faithful pause briefly, put their hands together and bow before going on their way.

A bus stops by the *dagoba* in Kalutara, the conductor jumps out and puts a coin in the slot in the temple wall, the passengers put their folded hands to their forehead, bow their heads and a few coins fly in the direction of the temple. Now everyone can continue on their journey with the Buddha's blessing.

HOW SIDDHARTHA FOUND ENLIGHTENMENT

The teachings of the Buddha originated in India about 2,500 years ago. The founder of the religion was an Indian prince by the name of Siddhartha who left his home aged 29 to seek a way out of life's eternal suffering as an ascetic. He found enlightenment aged 35, under a full moon in April/May while sitting beneath a Bo tree in

The Religious Complex
The religious festivals demonstrate clearly just how much Buddhism, Hinduism, Christianity and Islam are interlinked in Sri Lanka. The faithful from all four world religions join in a pilgrimage to Adam's Peak, the site of the 'sacred footprint' *(see pages 57 and 90)*, Hindus, Buddhists and Muslims also take part in the perahera to Kataragama *(see pages 74 and 91)*. Sinhalese and Tamils unite for April's New Year Festival.

Opposite: Wewurukannala Vihara
Bottom: puja at Kataragama

The Buddha's Visits
The Buddha is said to have visited Sri Lanka three times, including Kelaniya, Adam's Peak, Kataragama and Mahiyangana — all now pilgrimage sites.

Below: guardstone, Polonnaruwa
Bottom: the Bo Tree, Kandy

what is now Bodhgaya (Eastern India). This day is still the main Buddhist day of celebration (the Vesak festival; *see page 92*). From then on he toured the land as the Buddha, preaching and giving his blessing, until he died aged 80.

THE FOUR NOBLE TRUTHS

After the Buddha's death the Indian prince, Mahinda, brought the Buddhist teachings, the *dhamma*, to Sri Lanka in 250BC. Buddhism quickly became established as the state religion and has continued in its original form, Theravada Buddhism, to the present day. Some years later a sapling from the tree under which the Buddha sat in his quest for enlightenment was brought to Sri Lanka and planted in Anuradhapura: the sacred Bo tree. Since then Sri Lanka has often described itself as the land of Buddhism.

The Buddha is not worshipped as a god but as a human being who showed the way to enlightenment through wisdom – something which all human beings can achieve, provided they follow the Four Noble Truths.

Humans must first accept that suffering exists. The cause of all suffering is egoism and desire. Suffering can be overcome if desire ceases and the transitoriness of existence is accepted. This can be achieved by taking the Noble Eightfold

Way through meditation and adherence to the rules of life. On the way to nirvana, the final release from the cycle of rebirth, pity, equanimity, goodness, tolerance and compassion for all living creatures play a central role. Only in this way can *karma*, life's balance sheet of good and bad deeds, be influenced and the next existence be a better one.

BUDDHIST TEMPLES AND MONASTERIES

The traditional *dagobas* (also known as *stupas*) are visible from afar. These white, dome-shaped buildings with a gilded pinnacle are built within a square terrace to allow a staircase for each cardinal direction. The *dagoba* contains a relic of the Buddha or a priest, sometimes just a tiny part of a bone or a sacred text, and is traditionally sealed. Only in Kalutara is the inside of the domed structure accessible as it contains another *dagoba*, the actual reliquary.

Below: moonstone, Kataragama
Bottom: the Great Dagoba, Kalutara

Every monastery also has a statue hall with a figure of the Buddha, a residence for the monks or nuns and a Bo tree. In Sri Lanka Buddhas are portrayed in three positions. The standing Buddha usually holds up his hand as if giving a blessing (e.g. in Aukana), the seated Buddha is meditating, sometimes in the lap of a cobra, whose head reaches forward as protection, while the reclining Buddha is meditating or is already in a state of *nirvana*. If one foot is slightly withdrawn and the eyes closed, then this indicates that the Buddha is dead (e.g. Gal Vihara in Polonnaruwa)

MOONSTONES

By crossing a moonstone at the entrance to a Buddhist temple, a devotee undergoes a symbolic purification. The stone is semi-circular (imagine the other half hidden beneath the temple steps) and it represents the endless cycle of life

The 'Four Noble Truths' are immortalised in this 'rock doormat'. First you must step over the flames of fire – the state of the world – in the outer

Ancient Symbol
With their countless coloured sculptures of gods and human forms, Hindu temples (kovils) are a feast for the eyes. The swastika, an ancient Indian symbol for good luck, often adorns the entrance to the temples and also many homes. It has nothing to do with Hitler and the Nazis.

*Below: Ganapati and devotee
Bottom: the Goddess Kali*

ring. The next ring has animals representing the four stages of life: the elephant (for birth), the horse (old age), the lion (illness) and the bull (death and decay). The next circle of twisting plants symbolises lust and desire, the cause of suffering in life. Flying geese, symbols of wisdom in Sri Lanka, embody the retreat from lust and desire.

Finally, you reach the innermost ring and the lotus blossom, a symbol of purity and experience, the goal for those who continue the search for enlightenment.

The five steps of wisdom now lead the devotee into the inside of the temple and eventually to enlightenment.

HINDU DEITIES AND TEMPLES

After Buddhists, Hindus, with 18 percent of the population, represent the second largest religious group. They worship hundreds of gods, whom some say evolve from Brahma, the godhead. Hinduism is a very open religion without any fixed rules or dogmatic teaching. Even the Buddha appears in Hindu mythology as an incarnation of the Hindu god Visnu. Hindus also seek to break the cycle of rebirth through enlightenment. This release can be achieved through the worship of gods, asceticism, meditation or ritual *(see page 91)*. As the faithful can also be reborn as an animal, Hindus respect all creatures.

Guidance on the spiritual path is provided by the guru. In Sri Lanka the deities that are most frequently worshipped and portrayed are Skanda, the warrior god who rides a peacock, Ganapati, the god of wisdom and bringer of prosperity with his distinctive elephant's head, Visnu, the preserver of the universe, and Siva, the creator and destroyer.

Hindu gods also appear in many Buddhist temples. The architectural linkage between Buddhism and Hinduism began in the 11th century and has now reached the stage where in many Buddhist temples the Hindu god Skanda dominates the prayer hall, while a small Buddha is tucked away in a corner gathering dust. Buddhists also like to collect plus points for the next life by making offerings, but the Buddha regarded himself as a teacher. He is not to be worshipped in prayer and does not accept sacrifices. Because the many Hindu deities are given flowers, money and other gifts to ward off illness and accidents, over the centuries the two faiths have tended to merge.

Top: floral offerings
Middle: fire walker, Kandy
Bottom: Kandyan dancers

Dance-drama

Dance-dramas continue to be a vital part of Sri Lankan culture. Performers wearing frightening masks were once intended to keep epidemics at bay or to bestow a good harvest. With the aid of astrologers and exorcists the village community looked to the gods and demons.

The southwest coast of Sri Lanka continues to be the centre for traditional dance, puppet plays and masked carvings.

TEMPLE DANCES

The famous temple dances (Kandyan Dances), which originated in the Central Highlands region, can be seen every day in Kandy. The performance finishes with a dramatic fire-walking spectacle. Originally these rituals were part of sacrificial ceremonies, but now – combined with aspects of

traditional beliefs – they are even included in reservoir opening ceremonies. To the accompaniment of drums played by musicians decked out in red, white and silver, hundreds of dancers with extravagant head, breast and hip decorations parade past the bystanders for Kandy's *perahera*. They stamp their feet and roll their eyes, then twirl through the air, before coming to a graceful stop with fingers splayed.

Below: dancer and his mask
Bottom: drummers,
Kataragama

DANCES OF EXORCISM

Dubbed 'devil dances' by ill-informed Western observers, the ritual dances from the lowland region are wild, deafening and ecstatic. During the *sanni yakuma* ceremony, which is heavily exorcist in character, a victim is liberated from the grip of the powerful Prince Maha Kola and his 18 companions, the *sannis*.

The ritual lasts a whole night with neighbours and relatives in attendance. As the sun goes down, the ceremony begins with prayers to Lord Buddha and greetings to the demons outside the home of the 'possessed' – this could be a sick person, a fisherman whose nets are always empty or a farmer with a poor harvest. The chief exorcist invokes the chief demon, pulls faces and haggles over the patient, enticing the prince with a sacrificial cock or a coconut and a wild drumbeat.

Usually the next act explains through dance why Prince Maha Kola is so angry. His mother was killed by his father and the prince was put in an orphanage where he planned his revenge. To help out with the exorcism, the *palis*, 12 comical figures who look just as severe as the demons, are summoned. It is their job to make the audience and the victim laugh. The whole spectacle is actually more fun than fear-inducing. At the end Prince Maha Kola leaves the patient, who, as if in a trance, shakes off his tormentors. A fire-eater puts a burning torch in his mouth to swallow up the evil forces once and for all.

The *yakkas* are the underhand little devils who form part of the prince's entourage. Simply by looking, they can possess someone and can cause cholera, paralysis, poisoning, mental instability or death. The exorcists, however, are gradually dying out. Is there a shortage of *sannis* or *yakkas* or could it be that mere mortals can no longer find the fee – today's exorcists, plus their dancers charge between Rs 10,000 and 20,000.

Even so, the traditional dances do still sometimes take place, often in the area between Ambalangoda and Mirissa.

Kolam

Hotels regularly put on dance performances consisting of a mixture of colourful Kandy dances, masked ritual dancing and the traditional kolam dance-drama. The latter is a satirical portrayal of village life. The actors wear masks and represent different characters, such as the village officials, or relatives of the royal family – sometimes even yellow-faced and moustachioed European visitors.

PUPPET PLAYS

G. Wilson da Silva is a friendly old man who will wave you over cheerily for a cup of tea in his house in Ambalangoda. On the walls hang life-size puppets dressed in colourful clothes and wearing big smiles. Da Silva belongs to one of the few remaining families that has traditional links with puppetry. Like his father and grandfather he breathed life into the brightly coloured puppets. He would chip away at the soft *kaduru* wood with his hammer and chisel until heads and limbs took shape.

But it was clothes that gave character to people. Da Silva's wife made the often extravagant costumes which helped the audience to identify the characters: king and queen, beggar, clown and dancers, plus other well-known figures from contemporary Sri Lankan life and mythology.

Da Silva used to give two to three performances

Below: colourful puppets
Bottom: masked dancer

Murals

Sri Lanka's tradition of wall painting dates back to the 2nd century BC. There are reckoned to be three distinct styles of Sri Lankan mural painting. The first, early, category includes the female figures from the 5th-century palace of Sigiriya. The second is that of the Kandyan school (1750–1815), which finished with the British invasion but which has seen a revival due to renewed interest in Buddhist art. The third category is the decorative southern tradition, which details costume changes that occurred with each wave of invaders.

a month and was paid a relatively princely sum of about Rs 10,000 per performance, shared between the five or so members of his team. Without assistants, singers and musicians there can be no puppet play. For Da Silva, all that is behind him as he is now enjoying his retirement.

Unfortunately no one knows where the next generation of puppeteers will come from. Many of the older puppet-makers and operators kept their secrets to themselves. Sons often prefer to work as civil servants in Colombo or as guest workers in Kuwait, rather than follow in their father's footsteps. Puppet plays are still performed at festivals for tourists.

For further information ask at the Ceylon Tourist Board in Colombo or at the mask museum in Ambalangoda (see page 67).

MASK CARVING

A cobra head hangs above the bus driver, both eyes flash demonically in synchronisation with the indicators. When the driver brakes, the cobra's eyes light up – belief hand in hand with a lively imagination. The art of mask carving was for a long time closely connected with the dances performed to propitiate dangerous deities who are thought to control disease, but then it became tied up with the souvenir trade. In the workshop at the mask museum in Ambalangoda, for example, several men chisel away until a brightly painted deity, human or animal mask has been crafted from a large chunk of *kaduru* wood (from the *Nux vomica* tree). The process can take up to two weeks. It is still a manual skill but chemical paints have replaced natural dyes.

The best-known masks are those of the mythological bird *Garuda* and the cobra demon *Gara* (or *Garavaka*), the only benevolent demon who is often placed by a doorway to keep misfortune away. Eighteen masks represent the *sanni*, who can invoke all diseases. Demons can be recognised by their goggle eyes and their protruding tongues. As a general rule, the more impressive the head decoration, the more powerful the deity.

Mask of Gara

Special Events

POYA, PERAHERA AND PUJA

Every full moon day *(poya)* is a state holiday on which some important event in the life of the Buddha is recalled. Banks, theatres, cinemas and bars all close. Only in hotels is alcohol served to tourists (reception must be notified a day in advance). The most important full moon days are celebrated with a *perahera*, a procession in honour of the Buddha *(see page 92)*. For the daily religious ceremony, the *puja*, devout Buddhists look reverentially to their 'enlightened ones', Hindus to their gods. Prayers and music accompany the offering of sacrifices and in the Temple of the Tooth in Kandy the sacred shrine is opened. In Kataragama the faithful walk over glowing coals.

Below: offering a coconut, Kataragama
Bottom: procession, Kandy

PAYING HOMAGE TO THE SACRED TOOTH

The pushing and shoving starts at midday. The 11-day *Esala Perahera* in Kandy is approaching its climax. The wealthy and the tourists pay Rs 1,000 for the last seats in the stand in front of the Queen's Hotel. Thousands line the route. Some cling to street lamps in the hope of a glimpse of the most sacred Buddhist relic, a tooth from the mouth of the Buddha. The fact that it is only a replica that is carried through the streets

seems not to matter. As darkness falls, the procession of festively decorated elephants, dancers, acrobats and musicians starts to move. First whips crack, then come fire dancers, torch-bearers, flag-wavers, stilt-walkers, oboe players and drummers.

The Maligawa Tusker, the elephant bearing the Sacred Tooth in a golden casket, treads the white carpetway, followed by elephants bearing the insignia of the Hindu gods, Naha, Visnu, Kataragama and Pattini. For two hours the remaining elephants, draped with fabrics, bells and flashing lights, follow at a leisurely pace. The festival ends the next day with the water ceremony by the Mahaweli Ganga.

SUNRISE ON SRI PADA

It is a bitterly cold night sometime between January and April. The trail of lights snakes deep down into the valley, revealing the distance already covered. For the last and steepest of the 4,800 steps, each one of the many mountain climbers speeds up, as an orange glow is already brightening up the night sky. The red ball of fire soon appears on the horizon.

Luck plays a large part in seeing such a perfect sunrise. One Sinhalese man who has climbed Adam's Peak 100 times before says he has only seen such a splendid sunrise on three occasions.

Below: elephant, Navam Perehera, Colombo
Botttom: Adam's Peak

Sri Lankans undertake this arduous task for religious reasons. Buddhists, Hindus, Muslims and Christians have been making the pilgrimage up the 2,243m (7,177ft) mountain for over 1,000 years – always between December and May. At the busiest time in February the illuminated steps and the summit itself get very crowded.

Followers of all faiths regard the mountain as sacred. Muslims believe that Adam set foot on earth here after his expulsion from Paradise, but the footprint on the summit could also have been that of the Buddha, Siva or even St Thomas, the early apostle of India. Shivering with cold, the faithful welcome the sun with a prayer. Fruit, rice and money are offered to the relevant deity. Prayers ring out over the loudspeaker. Everyone has to clang the silver bell: one ring for each time they have climbed the mountain.

Skanda

The deity Skanda is also known by Hindus as the Tamil Murukan, and the Sanskritic deity Subramanyam, a son of Siva and Parvati, and by Buddhists as Kataragama Deviyo ('tutelary deity of Kataragama'). In his form at Kataragama he is usually regarded as the warrior god, but also variously represents compassion, justice and valour. Generally portrayed as a god with six faces and 12 arms, at the temple in Kataragama there is no image of the deity in the sanctum sanctorum but he is represented by his spear.

KATARAGAMA

One of the liveliest *peraheras* takes place at the end of July in Kataragama. Buddhists, Hindus and Muslims all regard Kataragama as a sacred site, where their gods will grant wishes and forgive sins. The Hindu temple is dedicated to Skanda. Ceremonials begin with ritual washing in the Menik Ganga. Only when body and clothes are purified is it safe to approach the shrine in the plain white Maha Devale temple. Followers of all faiths bring sacrificial offerings here. Even the festively decorated elephants must kneel in front of Skanda. The faithful break open coconuts on the entrance steps and the whole temple site glows with thousands of tiny oil lamps.

Observing the religious fervour of the pilgrims is a moving experience for outsiders. During the last few nights of this festival vows are made and kept, and acts of penance performed through ancient rituals. Pilgrims poke spears through one cheek skewering the tongue in the process. There is scorching sand to roll naked in and searing hot coals to walk barefoot over. The devotees themselves show little emotion, and some dance themselves into a trance-like state.

Devotee, Kataragama

Festival Calendar

January full moon
Duruthu Perahera, a colourful religious procession at the Kelaniya Temple near Colombo.

February full moon
Navam Perahera, a parade lasting two nights at the Gangaramaya Temple in Colombo.

4 February
Independence Day celebrated with parades and processions.

13/14 April
Sinhalese and Tamils celebrate **New Year**.

May full moon
Vesak Poya, street lights, decorations, torch-lit parades, puppet plays and free food from the street stalls to remember the three most important events in the life of the Buddha: his birth, enlightenment and death.

June full moon
Poson Poya, processions all over the island to remember the arrival of Buddhism on Sri Lanka in the 3rd century BC. The biggest ceremonies take place in Mihintale and Anuradhapura, where the first Buddhist teachings were passed on.

July/August
Various *peraheras*, the most famous being the one in **Kandy**, one of the greatest religious festivals in the world. Thousands of spectators and hundreds of decorated elephants, dancers and musicians take part in the processions, which continue day and night. Held in honour of the Sacred Tooth of the Buddha *(see page 89)*.

In **Kataragama**, a pilgrimage centre for Hindus, Buddhists and Muslims in the southeast, celebrations during the day and processions at night-time with trance dancers, fire-walkers and ancient self-chastisement rituals to the Hindu god, Skanda *(see page 74)*.

(see page 89)
(see page 74)

Poya Days
These ritual days for Buddhists fall at the time of the new moon and are considered the most auspicious days of the lunar month, and therefore the time of the most important services. On these days a devout Buddhist is expected to follow the Eight Precepts:
1. not to take life
2. not to take things not given
3. to abstain from sex
4. not to lie
5. not to become intoxicated
6. to fast after midday
7. not to take part in entertainment
8. to abstain from luxury

Tamil New Year

In **Dondra**, on the south coast, traditional dancing, processions and a traditional ceremony are held to pay homage to Visnu.

The most important Hindu festival, **Vel**, is held in Colombo in honour of Skanda with a procession in the Pettah bazaar quarter.

The exact dates for the peraheras in July/August are decided by astrologers and then made public in the spring.

October/November
Dipavali, the Hindu Festival of Lights is in honour of both Laksmi and Rama, the goddess of prosperity and the 7th *avatar* of Visnu.

December full moon
Start of the Sri Pada pilgrims' season. Adam's Peak (Sri Pada), the sacred mountain, attracts all faiths, Buddhists, Christians, Hindus and Muslims, right through until May *(see page 90)*.

End of the 9th month in the Islamic calendar
Sri Lanka's Muslims celebrate **Id-Ul-Fitr**, the end of Ramadan, with prayers. (Falls on 17 December 2001.)

Full moon days for 2002 fall on 28 January, 27 February, 28 March, 27 April, 26 May, 24 June, 24 July, 22 August, 21 September, 21 October, 20 November, 19 December.

Top: Vel festival, Colombo
Middle: Buddhist devotees, Colombo
Bottom: dancer, Navam Perehera. Colombo

FOOD AND DRINK

On the menu in most hotel restaurants are mainly Western dishes, but it is really not that great a challenge to sample the food in a local eating house or cafe *(kopi kade)*. It is traditional to eat with the fingers of your right hand, but Sri Lankans will make allowances for clumsy foreigners.

THE NATIONAL DISH

Sri Lanka's national dish is rice and curry. The basis for a proper curry is a carefully devised combination of herbs and spices, including caraway, coriander, cardamom, fennel seeds, onions, cloves, nutmeg, curry leaves, black and red pepper, mustard seeds, cinnamon, coconut flakes and/or coconut milk and chilli. From this collection of tasty, some hot, ingredients the Sri Lankan cook conjures up a white, red or brown, mild, thick, thin or dry curry, mixed with a few pieces of meat, fish, chicken, egg or vegetables. These are then served lukewarm in up to six or seven small dishes.

One thing is certain: it will be fiery hot. First it will burn the tongue and then set off an explosion of flavour in the mouth and throat. Sri Lankan cooking is one of the hottest in Asia.

To counter the hot flavour, take a mouthful of dry rice, or better still some yoghurt or cucumber. Sri Lankans will probably reach for the chilli paste, *pol sambol*, but foreigners will find this is pure dynamite. Take care with red chillies. The smaller they are, the hotter they will be.

If you do not like hot food then you do not need to miss out on the rice and curry. Many hotels serve a dish adapted to suit sensitive European palates. Side dishes are often mild and delicately flavoured. Try okra *(bandakka)*, pumpkin, pepper, beans, jackfruit and the smooth lentil paste known as *dhal*. Prices range from about 40p/60¢ in the street kitchens to £4 /$5.80 in hotel restaurants. Tourist hotels and restaurants by the coast also serve fresh seafood.

BREAKFAST AND SNACKS

Rotis are rather dry pancakes made from onion batter, eaten for breakfast with *sambol*, butter or marmalade or as a snack. The traditional Sri Lankan breakfast consists of pancakes called *hoppers* (crispy on the outside, soft inside). If there is an egg in the middle, it will be an *egg hopper*. *String hoppers* are tangled circles of steamed noodles, which when eaten with a meat curry taste delicious, even in the morning. *Kiribeth* is a type of milk rice, usually served with *jaggery,* a sweetner made from palm syrup.

If you want a snack on a day trip, call in at a roadside stall and try a vegetarian spring roll and *rolls* and *cutlis*, pockets of dough filled with cold chicken or fish. Be warned: the meatballs and round, often fish-filled rolls *(malu pan)* are fiendishly hot. One delicious dessert is *watalappam*, a coconut crème caramel. Curd is a yoghurt made from buffalo milk: try it with *jaggery*.

DRINKS

One wholesome thirst-quencher is *thambili*, the juice of the king coconut. Street sellers open the young fruit with a machete while you wait.

Even dedicated coffee drinkers quickly convert to tea, not just because the coffee is usually instant or some undefined, musty brew. Ceylon tea is a national treasure with an internationally recognised brand name. The quality of tea depends on the plant

Opposite: a curd stall, Konketiya

variety, the height of the plantation and the size of the dried tea leaf. After drying, grinding and fermenting, the leaves are sieved. The result will range between coarse 'O.P.' to 'dust' and 'fannings'. The best-known tea is the medium coarse *Broken Orange Pekoe*, which costs around £3.50/US$5 a kilo.

Another delicacy is Golden Tips, selected exclusively from the leaf tips. It can fetch around £14/US$20 a kilo. If you order tea, then it will be served with a lot of milk and even more sugar.

Freshly squeezed lime juice is a refreshing drink. All the internationally known soft drinks are widely available. The beer is good, but relatively dear for Sri Lanka. The local firewater is arrack, made from palm wine (toddy) and often mixed with fruit juice to make a delicious cocktail.

Treat tapwater with caution. Mineral water is available. Do not eat icecubes, ice cream, unpeeled fruit and salad to avoid a stomach upset.

SPICE GARDENS

You will have seen the plants somewhere before, but where? And the aroma! You will find the answer in one of the many spice gardens to the north and west of Kandy. A tour among the exotic flowers and everyday spices is a veritable treat for the senses.

The range of spices that this small island offers made it a highly desirable destination for Western seafarers centuries ago. Cinnamon, in particular, was very popular in Europe.

> **Tropical Fruit**
> There are many different varieties of mangoes and bananas. Rambutan, pineapples, oranges, pawpaws, guavas, melons, grapefruit and avocados are also plentiful. Fruit salad is served for breakfast practically everywhere.

Among the plants you will see are saffron, caraway, aniseed, cardamom, coriander, nutmeg and sometimes even cannabis. At a good spice garden you can find out how each of these precious flavours are used.

A close look at Sri Lankan plant life will reveal culinary surprises. Did you know, for example, that clove leaves produce a powder that is used for cleaning teeth, or that the green curry leaf *(karipatti)* gives the national dish its unmistakable aroma as well as its name? Also that many herbs and flowers are used in *ayurvedic* medicines *(see page 21)*? Neatly wrapped spices and jasmine, rose and sandalwood extract are on sale in the shop next door – and only slightly dearer than in the market.

Restaurant selection

The following are suggestions for the main destinations in this guide. They are listed according to three categories: $$$ = expensive, $$ = moderate, $ = inexpensive.

Colombo

Don Stanley's, 69 Alexandra Place, Colombo 7, tel: 686 486. First floor: lunch and evening buffet, snacks and cakes. First-class restaurant on the ground floor. $$–$$$.

Max's San Remo, 199 Union Place, Colombo 2, tel: 345 291. Mediterranean-style open-air setting with arcaded veranda and splashing fountain. Also an elegant – and more expensive – gourmet restaurant. $$.

Curry Leaf, Colombo Hilton, tel: 544 644. Local cuisine served in the hotel garden. Dinner only. $$.

Veranda, in the Galle Face Hotel, 2 Galle Face Centre Road, Colombo 3, tel: 541 010, fax: 541 072. Sea breeze and colonial setting. Even opens for breakfast. $$.

Ports of Call, Hotel Taj Samudra, 25 Galle Face Centre Road, Colombo 3. Open 24 hours. Good for breakfast. European/American/Sri Lankan buffet until 11am. $$.

Banana Leaf Restaurant, 86 Galle Road, Colombo 4, tel: 584 403. A friendly, traditional local restaurant where the food is served on banana leaves. $.

Palmyra Restaurant, Hotel Renuka, 328 Galle Road, Colombo 3, tel: 573 598. Famous for its Sri Lankan food and also good for Tamil dishes from Jaffna. $.

Seafish, 15 Sir Chittampalam A. Gardiner Mawatha, Colombo 2, tel: 326 915 and 431 826. Highly recommended Sri Lankan fish restaurant. $.

Pizza Factory in the Galadari Hotel. Pizzas baked at the back and shows on the stage. $.

Dosa King, 284 Galle Road, Colombo 3. Indian/Sri Lankan vegetarian restaurant. $.

Carnival Parlor, opposite Dosa King. Families and young people gather here to eat ice cream. $.

Summergarden, next to the art gallery in Ananda Coomaraswamy Mawatha, corner of C.W.W. Kannangara Mawatha (Cinnamon Gardens). Small, simple garden restaurant with view of the cricket pitch. $.

Kandy

If you are after an upmarket atmosphere, try the ballroom of the **Suisse Hotel**, and the **Queen's Hotel** (excellent club sandwiches and buffet lunch), both $$.

Kandyan Gate, 220 Senanayake Veediya. Pleasant and clean, serving Sri Lankan, Chinese and Western dishes, cakes and milkshakes. Tiny garden inside. $.

Avanhala, on the northern Sangaraja Mawatha, by the lake near Kandy Dance Show Hall. Open-air restaurant. $.

Lyon Cafe, 27 Peradeniya Road, near the station. A pleasant restaurant serving mainly Chinese food and some Sri Lankan dishes. $.

Negombo

Kopi Kade, 163 Lewis Place, near the Golden Star Beach Hotel. This small garden restaurant is one of the best places to try the local specialities, such as *koththu roti* or *egg hoppers*. $.

Anuradhapura

Crown Chinese Restaurant, 381 Dharmapala Mawatha. Cheap but reasonable Chinese and Sri Lankan fare. $.

Tempting rice and curry spread

Polonnaruwa

The restaurant in **Polonnaruwa Resthouse** *(see page 116)* is the ideal place for a curry in a pleasant atmosphere. $.

Nuwara Eliya

The Hill Club (not far from the Grand Hotel). If you are not dressed appropriately, then you can pick up a jacket and tie at the entrance. Meals in this colonial mansion range from genuine curry to European dishes. An experience not to be missed. $$$.

Restaurant Milano, New Bazar Street. Not an Italian in sight, but a good local restaurant serving Asian food. $.

Bentota/Alutgama

Terrena Lodge, River Avenue Road, Alutgama, tel: 034 75001. Small pavilions in the garden of a guesthouse by the banks of the river. Good food. Romantic spot. $.

All the hotels here have restaurants.

Hikkaduwa

Lounge bar and **pizzeria** in the Hotel Coral Gardens, Galle Road. Fresh seafood specialities and Western dishes lovingly prepared. $–$$.

German Bakery, 373 Galle Road. Best place for a hearty Western-style breakfast. Freshly baked bread. $–$$.

J.L.H. Beach Restaurant, 382/1 Galle Road. Some distance from the beach road. Small terrace. Western, Sri Lankan and Chinese dishes, plus fresh seafood. $.

Pop Starr Restaurant, near Moon Beam Hotel, Hikkaduwa-Narigama. A good place for snacks or seafood by the beach. $.

Galle

South Ceylon Restaurant, by the bus station near the entrance to the fort. A basic first floor restaurant for local people. Traditional food and very obliging waiting staff. $.

Parlour, next door. Ice cream cafe with tasty snacks. $.

Tangalla

Sun Shadow Beach Restaurant, by Tangalla beach. The sound of the waves is drowned out by reggae music. $.

More restaurants are to be found along the south coast road and in the hotels.

Matale

Aluvihara Kitchens, Kandy–Dambulala Road. This is some of the best Sri Lankan home cooking you will find, served in generous portions. Home-made chutneys, pickles and sweets also for sale. $.

Stuffed roti and tea for breakfast

SHOPPING

WOODCARVING

Sri Lankan woodcarvers are renowned for producing animals, Buddha figures, plates, candlesticks, lamps, vases and bowls made from ebony and teak. But you will also find souvenirs made from brass, bronze and copper, tea sets, cutlery and jewellery made from silver, basketware and raffia mats, lace and clothing, plus leather bags and suitcases. Popular souvenirs are batik clothing or wall decorations.

Lacquered goods range from painted walking sticks and letter openers, to musical instruments and toys.

BATIK

This method of fabric painting developed in Indonesia and has been widely used in Sri Lanka for about 50 years.

The desired pattern is first drawn on to the material. Before the first dying process, the areas of the material not intended to absorb that particular colour are painted with wax. The wax is later removed by boiling. The process is repeated with each new colour that is added.

Popular motifs include elephants, peacocks and Sigiriya murals.

OILS, SPICES AND TEA

Ayurvedic oils *(see page 21)* and herbs work wonders on certain ailments. Tea and aromatic spices are easy to fit into your luggage, but remember the duty-free limit of 3kg (6½lb) on tea.

PRECIOUS STONES

Sri Lanka's buried treasure includes rubies, sapphires, topaz, tourmaline, alexandrite, aquamarine, amethysts, garnets, spinel, zircon and moonstones. The island's reputation as home to a jewel hoard lured Arab seafarers and Chinese merchants, but the stones were often buried in muddy seams sometimes as far as 15m (50ft) underground.

Using traditional techniques, craftsmen in gemstone centres such as Ratnapura *(see page 60)* skilfully cut the sparkling gems, their value depending on colour, weight (carat), hardness and transparency. Probably the best-known stone to have been found in Sri Lanka, a 400-carat blue sapphire, now adorns the British crown.

Be wary of street dealers who offer you a 'special price'. Play safe and go to a government-approved jeweller. The State Gem Corporation *(see box below)* will test the stone for you and provide a certificate of authenticity. There is a showroom selling gems at fixed prices next door.

CLOTHING

Sri Lanka is a major centre for the manufacture of clothes for the Western market, including for chains such as Gap. Many of these are available locally at a fraction of the price back home. There is also a thriving market in fakes, which although not of the same quality as the originals are extremely good copies.

Gem Buying

If you are interested in buying gems, then address your queries to the **State Gem Corporation** (310 Galle Road, Colombo 3, tel: 01/574 274) or the **Ceylon Tourist Board**. They will supply the addresses of reputable dealers (those with state licences and who give a guarantee). You can if you wish bring a precious stone here for verification. Or you can buy direct from the State Gem Corporation who will issue a proof of quality certificate and a receipt. When exporting gems, the receipt must be shown at customs.

You might want to reflect on the fact that many of the clothes destined for Western markets and chains are produced in the Free Trade Zones, where workers are paid a pittance to work inhumanly long hours in very poor conditions.

SHOPPING CENTRES
Colombo
Laksala, 60 York Street, Colombo 1. A treasure trove for handicrafts. Monday to Friday 9.30am–5pm, Saturday 9.30am–4pm. Longer at weekends during the pre-Christmas period. Foreign currencies accepted. **Majestic City** and **Unity Plaza**, two spacious, air-conditioned shopping centres on Galle Road. Open until 10pm. There's almost anything you could want here, including a good bookshop. The shops in **Liberty Plaza**, Duplication Road, Colombo 3, are also well stocked. **Barefoot**, 704 Galle Road, Colombo 3, and **Lakmedura**, 113 Dharmapala Mawatha, Colombo 7, have textiles, crafts and *objets d'art*. You can browse and haggle to your heart's content with the **street market** traders in the Pettah, near the station on Olcott Mawatha and along Galle Road.

Worker in a batik factory near Aluvihara

Kandy
There are shoes, fabrics, leather goods and souvenirs galore in the central multi-storey **market hall**; tailors here will rustle up made-to-measure suits in no time, but do haggle.

Kandy is also famed for its wooden carved reliefs.

Negombo
There are many souvenir shops in the hotel shopping arcades, e.g. the Royal Oceanic, Blue Oceanic and Golden Star Beach. The small shops along **Lewis Place** towards the town centre are full of crafts, gold jewellery, leather, silks and batiks.

New arrivals should first check out the somewhat higher (non-negotiable) prices in the hotels and then try their luck with the street traders.

Bentota
Muthumuni Shop, 16 Galle Road, Kalawilawatta-Alutgama, tel: 034 76072. Gems and gold jewellery in all price ranges. Friendly and knowledgeable service.

Hikkudawa
There are good batiks at **Batik Studio and Workshop Sakura** on Waulagoda Road (turn off near the Reefcomber Hotel).

NIGHTLIFE

Most nightlife in Sri Lanka is to be found in Colombo, where it is centred on the top hotels. Clubs are normally open seven days and late into the night (on *poya* days no drinks can be served). Expect to pay a cover charge of a few hundred rupees. Dress style is generally smart casual. There is a growing number of pubs and bars.

Colombo

Classical Sri Lankan and Western theatre and changing exhibitions (painting, photography, fashion and furniture) at the **Lionel Wendt Theatre**, Guildford Crescent, Colombo 7, tel: 695 794.

Live music until early in the morning at the **Saxophone Jazz Club** (46B Galle Road, tel: 334 700).

Top nightclubs and discos are the **Blue Elephant** in the Hilton (tel: 544 644) and **Valentino's** in the Hotel Galadari. Currently the trendiest club in town is **Cascades** at the Hotel Lanka Oberoi (tel: 320 001). If these are full then the following are worth checking out: **Colombo 2000** also at the Galadari; **Cyclone** at 29 Maitland Crescent (tel: 075 378 017); **The Library** at the Trans Asia Hotel (tel: 544 200); and **Legends** at Magestic City.

Kandy

Roots & Leaves, in the Tree of Life Hotel, Yahalatenna, Barigama, Werellagama-Kandy, tel: 08 499 777. Dancing every Friday and Saturday. Located 13km (8 miles) from Kandy.

Negombo

Honky Tonk Bar (near the Sunflower Beach Hotel). Beer, fried rice and rock music for night-owls. The latest venue is the **Underwater Disco** in the Hotel Ocean Garden (tel: 031 77309).

Nuwara Eliya

The **bar** in the **Grand Hotel** is really cosy. Enjoy a drink beside the open fireplace, followed by a game of billiards.

Bentota

There is always something going on at **Club Intersport** north of Bentota Beach Hotel, tel: 034 75178. It is a watersports centre during the day, but there is more fun after sunset in the form of open-air discos, karaoke, music videos and shows.

The luxury 5-star **Eden Hotel**, Kaluwamodara-Beruwala, tel: 034 76075–6 is the place to be seen. Entertainment for hotel guests and visitors includes magicians, masked balls and dancing competitions.

Hikkudawa

Plenty of activity along the main road and in the beach restaurants during the season. If that is not enough, then try the **discotheque** in the **Coral Gardens Hotel** (Galle Road, tel: 09 77422), the finest of Hikkaduwa's hotels which also has bars, restaurants and a shopping centre.

Karaoke Bars

Now very popular in Colombo, try: **Showboat**, 104 Reid Avenue, Colombo 4, tel: 596 958.

Not noted for the quality of the food, Showboat is still popular because of its state-of-the-art Karaoke Lounge (with English, Thai, Korean, Chinese and Japanese songs) and its MTV lounge providing daily movies and sports coverage.

Hilton Karaoke, tel: 544 644.

A wide range of music, a well-stocked bar, and an easy-going atmosphere make this one of the most popular karaoke bars around.

ACTIVE HOLIDAYS

SWIMMING, DIVING AND DEEP-SEA FISHING

Many holidaymakers come to Sri Lanka to enjoy swimming in the warm coastal waters. During the southwesterly monsoons (May to September/October), the beach is narrower, the sea choppy and swimming is only possible in a few places such as in Unawatuna Bay.

Good diving places include coral banks and old shipwrecks in the Great and Little Basses Reef *(see page 73)*, off Hambantota, Galle, Hikkaduwa, Negombo, Chilaw and Kalpitiya on the south and west coast. Four hours of deep-sea diving or fishing in Hikkaduwa costs about Rs 4,000 per boat (3–5 persons) with equipment. Diving schools are usually owned by hotels. Courses by PADI-approved instructors cost up to £240/US$350 a week. Take medical certification.

SURFING, WATER-SKIING AND SAILING

Wherever Australians congregate there will be good surfing opportunities, for example in Hikkaduwa-

Spectacular palm trees at the beach

Narigama (winter only). Many hotels by the coast offer a good range of watersports.

Even inland you can hire water skis, e.g. on the River Benota. Trips by *oruwa* (outriggers) to the offshore islands and lagoons are often available from fishermen: negotiate the price before you set off. Usually moored in Galle harbour are yachts on the look-out for crew (experience not always necessary: contact the yachting office at the harbour or consult the hotel noticeboards).

THE GLASS-BOTTOMED BOAT

Trips out to sea in a glass-bottomed boat are available in Hikkaduwa between November and April. However, these have damaged the coral so severely that much of it has now died and visitors are strongly advised not to take them *(see page 67)*.

IN THE MOUNTAINS AND IN THE JUNGLE

Kandy and Nuwara Eliya are the best starting points for walks and day trips, ideally between February and May or during August and September. There are a number of nature reserves with

footpaths (for example Hakgala Botanical Gardens, *see page 56*). Up in the mountains strong footwear, jumpers and anoraks are recommended. For longer walks, carry a water bottle.

In the winter, Adam's Peak *(see page 57)* can be crowded with pilgrims. In the rainy season wear sturdy shoes if walking in the rainforests to keep the flukes away from the ankles. Most excursions can be undertaken independently.

The *Trekkers Guide to Sri Lanka* (Colombo, 1994), from local bookshops, recommends routes and has useful tips.

Cricket

This sport is a national passion. The season runs Spetember–April and some clubs will accept temporary foreign members. Contact:

Nondescripts Cricket Club, 29 Maitland Place, Colombo 7, tel: 95293.

Broomfield Cricket and Athletic Club, Reid Avenue, Colombo 7, tel: 914 119.

Dikoya and Maskeliya Cricket Club, tel: 051 2216.

Uva Club, Bailey Road, Badulla, tel: Badulla 216.

GOLF

There is an 18-hole course in Nuwara Eliya (Nuwara Eliya Golf Club, tel: 052 22835). The Royal Golf Club in Colombo (tel: 01 695 431) also has an 18-hole course.

CYCLING

For organised rides through rubber estates and downhill rides through tea estates contact **Adventure Sports Lanka (PVT) Ltd**, 12A Simon Hewavitharane Road, Colombo 3, tel: 074 713 334, fax: 01 577 951, e-mail: adventur@srilanka.net

For the less active

Courses in batik are given by experienced artists in their studios in Panadura (Bandulla Fernando), Kandy (Gunatillaka Batics, Rajapihilla Mawatha) and Matara (Jez-Look Batics, Jezima Mohamed, 12 Yehiya Mawatha).

Many meditation centres run courses for Europeans interested in Buddhist philosophy. One such centre is in Kandy-Nilambe (near Galaha: no power or phone, about £14/US$20 a week, reservation not necessary). More details: The International Buddhist Research and Information Centre, 380/9 Sarana Road (off Bauddhaloka Mawatha), Colombo 7, tel: 01 689 388 (bookshop, open 9am–5pm).

In the south of the capital, Dr Pilapitiya, director of the National Ayurveda Research Institute, runs a clinic (Vedamadura, Kesbewa, tel: 01 504 362). Two clinics, one by the coast and one in the mountains, offer massages with oils, herbs and special diets: Lotus Villa in Ahungalla, tel: 09 64082, fax: 64088, and Ayurvedic Healthcare Resort, Greystones Villa, Diyatalawa, Uva District.

GETTING MARRIED IN SRI LANKA

Like other islands in the Indian Ocean, Sri Lanka has become a popular place for couples from colder latitudes to get married. Although it is possible to pre-book everything through a tour operator, it is also possible to make your own arrangements. A marriage with priests and a ceremonial sari for the bride, and retinue, the traditional guard's costume from Kandy for the groom, plus Kandyan dancers and an elephant ride, can be arranged for about £275/US$400. Many hotels on the southwest coast organise weddings if given plenty of notice.

PRACTICAL INFORMATION

Getting there

BY AIR

The main airport in Colombo is Bandaranaike International Airport, more commonly known as Katunayake.

The national carrier, Sri Lanka Airlines (UL), has a network of international flights spanning most major destinations.

Flights for Sri Lanka from Europe depart from London, Amsterdam, Frankfurt, Paris, Rome, Vienna and Zurich, and take between 10 and 14 hours.

Bandaranaike airport is situated 35km (22 miles) north of Colombo. Due to the chaotic traffic situation, a taxi needs about an hour to get from the airport to the city centre (fare into the city about Rs 700 per taxi).

Bus nos. 240 and 187 run to the city's bazaar quarter. There are also radio taxis, e.g. Quick Cabs, tel: 502 888 (about Rs 25 per km). Airport information is available, e.g. Lionair, Asian Aviation Centre, Ratmalana Domestic Airport, tel: 622 622, 635 163, 612 735, fax: 611 540.

There is a room reservation office run by the Ceylon Tourist Board at the airport. The *bureau de change*, also at the airport, is usually open 24 hours. If not, it opens when planes arrive. Because of the civil war, for security reasons you may have to put up with certain formalities.

Independent travellers must confirm their return flight no later than two days before departure (by phone with the relevant airline in Colombo). You should have your reconfirmation code ready.

For flight information tel: 01 452 281, 452 282, 452 911. Amairport Katunayake, tel: 073 2677; Sri Lanka Airlines, tel: 073 5555.

Getting around

BY HIRE CAR

Driving in Sri Lanka is not for the faint-hearted. Sri Lankan roads are very congested and poorly maintained, with pot holes, unsecured roadsides, dust and gravel tracks, plus the added hazard of stray animals.

It is a far better bet to hire a car with an English-speaking chauffeur. He will usually take care of everything and can give advice about accommodation and restaurants. This service is well worth the extra money (usually more than Rs 100 per day) on top of the car rental charges.

A hire car without a driver for a week with a limitation on mileage starts at about Rs 5,500. Avis, the international care hire company, has a branch in Sri Lanka (McKinnon's Travel, 4 Leyden Bastion Road, Colombo 1, tel: 01 329 887–8, fax: 522 351). An international driver's licence is required with the minimum age 25. Driving is on the left and the road signs are in English.

The Automobile Association of Ceylon is at 40 Sir Macan Markar Mawatha, Galle Face, Colombo 3, tel: 01 421 528–9, fax: 446 074.

MOTORCYCLE

Gold Wing Motors (125 Nawale Road, Havahenpita, Colombo 5, tel: 580 597 and 589 963, fax: 508 124) rent out 125–250cc motorbikes for Rs 400 per day. Helmets are obligatory. Any insurance is usually inadequate – wherever there is any doubt about liability, the driver pays.

BUS

The rickety red, silver and yellow buses are by far the cheapest way to get around both in town and in the country. It costs two rupees to climb aboard and from then on it is every person for themselves, one neighbour's elbow in the ribs and another's head against a shoulder. When it is your time to get off you will have to fight your way slowly to the exit with a musical accompaniment playing in the background. Buses stop at bus stops, but will also pull over in response to hand signals.

Overland buses serve every distant corner of the country. For Rs 30, for example, a passenger can travel 150km (90 miles). Private companies operate thousands of often air-conditioned minibuses. There is rarely a timetable, but the rules are simple. When the bus is full, off you go. Even so, this is still the quickest way to get around.

If you turn down the opportunity to take a bus ride then you are missing out on a typical aspect of everyday life in Sri Lanka. Once you are inside, do not be too quick to occupy one of the two free places behind the driver. These are reserved for, or should be offered to, monks.

The routes in Colombo are detailed in the monthly *Travel Lanka* and *Arjuna's A–Z Street Guide*. Enquire at the Ceylon Tourist Board about special tourist buses.

Colombo

Bus station on Olcott Mawatha 300m (330 yards) from the station, tel: 581 120 (Ceylon Tourist Board reservations and minibuses), tel: 328 081 (Information) at bus station.

Kandy

Air-conditioned, inter-city express buses run from the bus station several times a day.

RAIL TRAVEL

Presently, trains only run from Colombo to the south and to the hill country (Kandy). Trains to the north (Jaffna) and to the east (Trincomalee) have stopped. Long-distance trains have air-conditioned first-class compartments (with a panoramic carriage at the end of the train). First-class tickets can be booked (ideally a few days beforehand on *poya* days and similar festivals). It is also necessary to book for first-class couchettes. For most trains with second- and third-class compartments, simply be at the station in good time and then join the throng. A three-hour train journey costs about Rs 60. Keep your ticket – it will be collected when you leave the station.

Passengers waiting for the train at Colombo Fort station

Travelling by train on the 1,400-km (900-mile) network can be slow and uncomfortable. Some of the tracks still date from the colonial era, and there are frequent delays.

The train journey from Colombo to Badulla (9 hours) is highly recommended because of the splendid views. The line through the highlands and permanently green mountain ranges and waterfalls run beside Bible Rock and along the Mahaweli Ganga valley. At the very least travel on one of the following sections: Colombo–Kandy, Kandy (Nanu Oya)–Nuwara Eliya or Nuwara Eliya–Ella.

For a piece of nostalgia enquire about the possibility of a ride on the steam-hauled 'Viceroy Special'. It runs twice a week during the high season. Colombo to Kandy costs US$190 for a two-day ticket, including lunch, hotel accommodation and excursions. The train can be hired for groups.

For information and reservations contact J.F. Tours & Travels, 42 Glenaber Place, Colombo 4, tel: 01 589 402, 587 996, 583 387, fax: 583 696, 580 507. The Railway Tourist Information Centre is at Fort Railway Station, Colombo 1, tel: 01 435 838 and 434 215.

Colombo
Colombo Fort Station, Olcott Mawatha. For information, tel: 434 215, 435 838.

Kandy
The station is on S.W.R.D. Bandaranaike. Six trains every day to and from Colombo. In winter the 'Viceroy Special' runs twice a week via Colombo to the coast *(see above)*.

Nuwara Eliya
The station is about 7km (4 miles) away in Nanu Oya and can be reached by bus or taxi.

TAXI
When travelling in the yellow, red or dark blue taxis, the meter (if fitted) should always be switched on, otherwise you will have to put your negotiating skills to the test – and before getting in. Prices within urban areas are about Rs 25 per kilometre.

A trip in a trishaw (or *tuk-tuk*) will be cheaper. Drivers of these colourful three-wheel taxis with two-stroke engines initially ask foreign visitors for three to five times above the normal price. Reckon to pay about Rs 15 per kilometre, or Rs 250 for a half-day excursion

Cycling
The best way to visit the ruins at Anuradhapura and Polonnaruwa is by bike. Rental charges are Rs 75–100 per day.

TRAVEL AGENTS
Travel agents who organise guided tours by coach or private car include: **Aitken Spence Travels Ltd**, Vauxhall Towers, 305 Vauxhall Street, Colombo 2, tel: 345 112, fax: 422 381. e-mail: astravel@aitkenspence.lk
Jetwing Travels Ltd, 46/26 Navam Mawatha, Colombo 2, tel: 345 700, fax: 075 345 710.
e-mail: jettrav@sri.lanka.net
Lanka Sportsreizen, 211 Hospital Road, Kalubowila, tel: 824 955, fax: 826 125.
Mackinnons Travels Ltd, 4 Leyden Bastian Road, Colombo 1, tel: 329 887, fax: 440 881.
e-mail: mtl@keells.com
Quickshaws Tours Limited, 3 Kalinga Place, Colombo 5, tel: 583 133, fax: 587 613.
e-mail: quiktur@lankacom.net
Walkers Tours Ltd, 120 Glennie Street, Colombo 2, tel: 327 540, fax: 447 087.
e-mail: dreamhole1@walkers.slt.lk

AIRLINE OFFICES

Aeroflot, North Wing, Taj Samudra Hotel, 25 Galle Face Centre Road, Colombo 3, tel: 433 062, fax: 445 919.

Air Maldives, 81 York Street, Colombo 1, tel: 343 710, fax: 342 295.

Balkan Bulgarian, 321 Union Place, Colombo 2, tel: 451 300, fax 451 307.

Cathay Pacific, 186 Vauxhall Street, Colombo 1, tel: 334 145, fax: 423 406.

Emirates, Hemas House, 75 Braybrooke Place, Colombo 2, tel: 300 200, fax: 300 219.

Gulf, 11 York Street, Colombo 1, tel: 434 662, fax: 422 641.

Indian Airlines, Bristol Complex, 4 Bristol Street, Colombo 1, tel: 326 844.

Kuwait, Cargills Building, Sir Baron Jayatilleka Mawatha, Colombo 1, tel: 430 525, fax: 449 080.

Lauda, Jetwing House, 46/26 Navam Mawatha, Colombo 2, tel: 3457 00, fax: 345 725.

Oman, Trans Asia Hotel, Colombo 2, tel: 544 200, fax: 447 906.

PIA, 342 Galle Road, Colombo 3, tel: 573 475, fax: 576 880.

Qatar, 61 EML Building, W.A.D. Ramanayake Mawatha, Colombo 2, tel: 300 195, fax: 300 407.

Royal Jordanian, 40A Kumaratunga Munidasa Mawatha, Colombo 3, tel: 301 621, fax: 301 620.

Saudi Arabian, Aeroworld Pvt Ltd, 466 Galle Road, Colombo 3, tel: 576 078, fax: 577 241.

Singapore, 315 Vauxhall Street, Colombo 2, tel: 300 757, fax: 300 756.

Sri Lankan Airlines, Main Ticket Office: 2-2 West Block, World Trade Centre, Colombo 1, tel: 073 3300, fax: 073 5330. Reconfirmation: tel: 073 5500. Flight enquiries: tel: 073 2377.

Thai, 48 Janadhipathi Mawatha, Colombo 1, tel: 438 050, fax: 438 895.

Facts for the visitor

TRAVEL DOCUMENTS

Nationals from over 50 countries, including the United Kingdom, do not require a visa to stay in Sri Lanka for a period of 30 days, if arriving as tourists. It is possible to extend this for another 30 days, in which case you must apply to the Sri Lankan Embassy in London or to the Department of Immigration and Emigration in Colombo (Marine Drive, Colombo 1, tel: 01 436 353, 436 354).

Visitors are allowed to bring in personal equipment such as radios, sports equipment, laptop computers and photographic equipment. Importing

Bus station, Badulla

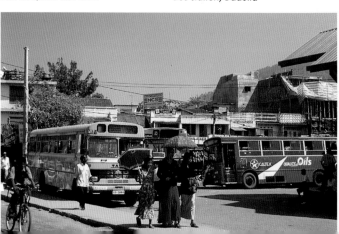

illegal drugs, fire-arms or pornography of any form is an offence. If you are bringing in over US$5,000, it should be declared at customs on arrival.

Duty-free allowances permit up to 2 litres of spirits, 2 bottles of wine, 200 cigarettes or 50 cigars, and perfume in a quantity for personal use.

TOURIST INFORMATION
Sri Lanka (Ceylon) Tourist Board
In the UK
22 Lower Regent Street, London SW1Y 4QD, tel: 020 7930 2627, fax: 020 7930 9070. Open Monday to Friday, 9am–5pm.
In the US
1 World Trade Centre, Suite 4667, New York, NY 10048, tel : 212 432 7156, fax: 212 524 9653, e-mail: ctbUSA@anlusa.com

In Sri Lanka
Colombo
Ceylon Tourist Board, 78 Galle Road, Colombo 3, tel: 437 059, 437 060, 437 952, 437 055, fax: 437 953. Open 9.30am–12.30pm and 2–5pm. Opposite Hotel Lanka Oberoi; information desk at the airport and the station.

An accommodation guide listing hotels and guesthouses (updated every six months) can be obtained from the Ceylon Tourist Board. Also available in most good hotels are the magazines *Travel Lanka* and *Explore Sri Lanka* (monthly), which contain useful addresses and tips.

The Ceylon Tourist Board and the Tourist Guide Lecturers' Association in Colombo (tel: 01 595 212, 864 044) can supply English-speaking guides.
Kandy
Travel Information Centre, Headman's Lodge, 3 Deva Veediya, tel: 222 661.
Negombo
Tourist Information, Lewis Place.

DIPLOMATIC REPRESENTATION
British High Commission, 190 Galle Road, Colombo 3, tel: 01 437 336/43, fax: 430 308, e-mail: bhc@eureka.lk United States Embassy, 210 Galle Road, Colombo 3, tel: 01 448 007, fax: 437 345.

TIME
Sri Lankan time is 6 hours ahead of Greenwich Mean Time. When it is noon in Sri Lanka, it is 6am in London and 1am in New York.

ELECTRICITY
230-240V AC. You can usually borrow an adapter for three-pin plugs.

CURRENCY AND EXCHANGE
The Sri Lankan rupee is divided into 100 cents. About 128 rupees (Rs) equal £1 and Rs 88 equal US$1. At the airport the Bank of Ceylon runs a bureau de change that is open round the clock. It also has an office in Colombo Fort (York Street, daily 9am–6pm, Saturday, Sunday, public holidays 9am–4pm). Banks in Kandy and other towns usually close at 1pm.

Some banks have ATMs which issue cash against credit cards (mainly Visa and American Express), e.g. Hong Kong Bank in Colombo and in Kandy. Most hotels change cash and travellers' cheques and also accept credit cards.

TIPPING AND TAXES
With an average monthly income of about £30/US$43, Sri Lankans welcome tips, large or small. A tax of between 16 and 21 percent is added to all hotel and restaurant prices.

OPENING TIMES
Shops are usually open Monday to Friday 9am–5pm (often until 7pm in Colombo); many also open on Saturday morning. In tourist areas, shops stay open until late at night.

Offices open Monday to Friday 8.30am–4.30pm (with irregular midday breaks).

National and local museums are open daily (except Friday) 9am–5pm, **archaeological museums** daily (except Tuesday) 8am–5pm.

> ### Holidays
> Few other nations have as many public holidays as Sri Lanka. Every full moon day *(or poya, see page 92)* is a religious holiday. Religious festivals *(see pages 92–3)* are always celebrated in grand style.
> National holidays: 15 January (Tamil Harvest Festival), 4 February (National Day), Good Friday, 1 May, 22 May (National Heroes' Day), 26 September (Bandaranaike Remembrance Day), 25 December (Christmas).

POST, TELEPHONE AND FAX

Airmail letters to Europe cost Rs 20, postcards Rs 15. They normally take between a week to 10 days to arrive, but occasionally delivery takes much longer. If you have a phone card, then you can phone from the General Post Office (GPO) in Colombo Fort round-the-clock. Cards can be bought at post offices and in many other shops. There are numerous other small shops in Colombo Fort, offering fax and phone services. Calls to Europe between 6am and 10pm cost from about Rs 160 per minute, between 10pm and 6am from Rs 110. Phone calls from hotels can cost considerably more.

In many of the main tourist resorts, a direct dial call can be made from telephone kiosks (with phone cards).

For international enquiries, dial 134 if you are calling within Colombo or 324 144 or 329 792 if you are calling from outside Colombo.

General Post Office, Janadhipathi Mawatha, Colombo 1, tel: 01/326 203 and 323 140, open daily 24 hours. The *poste restante* counter in the GPO is open 7am–9pm. Telegrams accepted from 7am to 8pm.

Most other post offices are open Monday to Friday 7am–3pm; many are also open on Saturday morning.

Internet

Visitors can surf the internet and send e-mail at any of the independent cyber-cafes in Colombo at rates starting from Rs 130 per hour, or otherwise at the British Council (49 Alfred House Gardens, Colombo 3, tel: 581 171, fax: 587 079) for Rs 750 for 10 hours. Try also: The café@inter.net, 491 Galle Face Road, Colombo 3, tel: 508 266, fax: 508 616, e-mail: cafe@isplanka.lk

MEDICAL MATTERS

It is recommended that travellers have standard vaccinations against tetanus, diphtheria and polio. Cholera immunisation is also suggested. Anti-malaria tablets prescribed by your doctor should be started about a week before you plan to arrive and continued for at least two weeks after you return, depending on the brand you have been prescribed.

It is advisable to bring mosquito repellents with you although citronella oil, readily available in Sri Lanka, is an effective natural repellent. The best way to avoid malaria is to wear suitable clothing (long-sleeved T-shirts, trousers and socks) from sunset to sunrise. If you plan to stay in inexpensive hotels, you may be glad to have a travel mosquito net.

The heat is intense, especially in the afternoon when the sun is best avoided altogether. Use a maximum protection sunblock or tanning lotion that has a high protection factor.

If you do go out in the midday sun, take a large hat or a parasol (Sri Lankans often use umbrellas).

It is vital to drink plenty of fluids in the humid Sri Lankan climate to avoid dehydration. Do not drink tap water unless you are sure it has been boiled. Many restaurants claim their table water is boiled, but to avoid any risk, stick to bottled water or bottled or canned fruit juices and carbonated drinks. Coconut water *(thambili)* drunk straight from the shell is a great thirst-quencher, widely available and has remarkable rehydration properties.

If you start feeling the effects of sun stroke, such as nausea, dizziness and headaches, find somewhere shady to rest, drink something cool, take some salt and bathe your face in cool water.

Diarrhoea can wreck a holiday, so take precautions. Wash and peel fruit, and don't eat raw vegetables. If you are prone to stomach upsets, carry Lomatil or Pepto-Bismal with you.

Most hotels have a doctor on call, and most embassies can provide a referral list.

Medical attention is available from many private hospitals, or from the state-owned **Colombo General Hospital** (Regent Street, Colombo 8, 24-hour service, tel: 691 111, 693 184–5, ambulance: 422 222). It has the most advanced cardiology unit on the island and provides medical attention free to Sri Lankans. Foreigners are required to pay for certain services. There are general hospitals in Kandy (tel: 08 23337), Negombo (tel: 031 22261) and Galle (tel: 09 32276). Although many doctors have British qualifications, state hospitals have poor facilities and crowded wards.

Private hospitals are well staffed, and are generally competently run and also comfortable. In the capital, you can choose from the following:
Asiri Hospital, 181, Kirula Road, Colombo 5, tel: 508 766. One of the better hospitals, with 24-hour service and laboratory testing.

Central Hospital, 37 Horton Place, Colombo 7, tel: 696 411/2. Offers medical treatment at a reasonable cost.
General, Regent Street, Colombo 7, tel: 691 111. Excellent laboratory but not a comfortable place for a long stay.
Nawaloka, 23 Sri Sugathodaya Mawatha, Colombo 2, tel: 544 444. Good laboratory and competent staff, reasonably comfortable rooms.

In an emergency, especially on a Sunday, first telephone to find out which specialists they have on call and select your hospital accordingly.

Pharmacies

Most popular, conventional medicines are available in chemists, with the best range to be found in Cargill's Department Store in Colombo Fort. The Asiri Hospital has a pharmacy that is open quite late, and the Osusala Pharmacy in Colombo (tel: 694 716) is open 24 hours.

Ayurvedic centres

Homeopathic and traditional South Asian medicine *(ayurvedic)* is an alternative option available at hotels and health centres *(see page 21)*:
Aida's Ayurveda Hotel, Bentota, tel: 034 71136–9.
Ayurveda Medical Centre, Diyatalawa, tel: 057 22032.
Ayurveda Walauwa, Bentota, tel: 034 75374.
Barberyn Reef Hotel, Beruwela, tel: 034 76036.
Blue Oceanic Hotel, Ethukala, Negombo, tel: 031 79000.
Culture Club, Kandalama, Dambulla, tel: 066 31822.
Deer Park Hotel, Giritale, Polonnaruwa, tel: 027 46272.
Giritale Hotel, Giritale, tel: 027 46311.
Government Ayuvedic Hospital, Colombo, tel: 695 855.
Robinson Club, Paradise Island,

Aluthgama, tel: 034 75167.
Royal Oceanic Hotel, Ethukala, Negombo, tel: 031 79000.
Siddhalepa Ayurveda Hospital, Mount Lavinia, tel: 738 622.
Siddhalepa Ayurveda Health Resort, Pothupitiya, Wadduwa, tel: 034 96967/0744 284 996.
Tree of Life, Werellagama, Kandy, tel: 08 499 777.
Villa Ocean View, Wadduwa, tel: 034 32463.

ADMISSION PRICES

You can buy visitors' permits for the 'Cultural Triangle' either in Colombo (Central Cultural Fund, 212/1 Bauddhhaloka Mawatha, Colombo 7, tel: 01 500 733, 587 912) or on the spot in Anuradhapura, Polonnaruwa, Sigiriya and Kandy. An all-in ticket costs about £23/US$33.

You can buy separate tickets for the historic sites, but if you intend to see as many as possible the all-in ticket is much better value.

Admission prices for other temple complexes vary between Rs 30 and 60

Photography

Sri Lankans are generally happy to be photographed, as long as they are asked in advance. A little chat is also appreciated. The local people are often thrilled if you ask them for their address and promise them a copy of your snap. To avoid offending people's feelings refrain from taking photographs of Sri Lankans washing by the roadside, in the river or beneath a waterfall. In temples and monasteries always ask first. At some tourist sights visitors must buy a photography permit. If you buy an all-in ticket for the 'Cultural Triangle' then this is included.

Colour print films are available all over Sri Lanka, but slide films are expensive – if you can find them. Film development is relatively cheap, but quality is variable.

and that will cover everything. But at World's End *(see page 56)*, for example, the government has decided to take advantage of tourists and charges an extortionate admission charge, usually payable in dollars.

CLOTHING

Give careful consideration to the clothing that you take. It is very important to protect your skin both from the sun and from mosquitoes *(see* Medical Matters *above)*. Sri Lankans are used to seeing men wearing shorts, but they still regard them as something worn by schoolboys.

When travelling, light loose-fitting clothes are the most comfortable, but if you plan to go up into the hill country then a jumper, an anorak and good walking shoes are vital.

Air-conditioned hotels, restaurants and cars can sometimes feel chilly, so it is a good idea to have a lightweight top easily accessible. It is always important to dress appropriately when entering a temple.

CRIME

Sri Lanka is a safe country for travellers. If anything untoward does happen, contact the Tourist Police: Fort Police Station, Bank of Ceylon Mawatha, Colombo 1, tel: 433 342, 433 744. Tourist police: tel: 432 635, Police: tel: 433 333.

The often-bulging wallets of tourists are a great temptation for conmen and wheeler-dealers. Whenever you are out and about, then 'buyer beware' is the motto. If, for example, when you are wandering among the ruins at Anuradhapura, you are offered what appears to be an ebony carving for Rs 800, it could be simply cheap wood painted black or else a low-quality slow seller. If you bought a map for a historic site in Cargill's Department Store, then you would be paying a fifth of what the street traders ask at the entrance. When you are strolling along the beach and you see suntan lotion for sale at incredibly low prices, this should arouse your suspicion. Probably only the plastic bottle is genuine. Also, distances given by trishaw drivers are often greatly exaggerated.

STREET TRADERS, TOUTS AND BEGGARS

You are sitting on the beach, camera at the ready to capture the beautiful sunset for your holiday album. Why then is the old Sinhalese woman standing directly between you and the setting sun waving her collection of colourful sarongs at you. She is certainly not doing it to annoy you. It is the same with the young man with the python round his neck who plays exactly the same tune day in day out.

There are hotels where guards are employed to keep traders and touts away from guests. However, can you blame the locals for wanting to do a bit of business with the tourists?

A different sort of problem exists in the tourist citadels and by the south and southwest coast. Keeping the many self-appointed guides at bay can be a tedious business. It is probably better to find a former teacher who can speak good English, has a vehicle, plenty of local knowledge and will stick to the negotiated prices.

The friendly overhelpfulness of touts is designed to make you feel obliged to part with your money. They will come up with many convincing stories. Among the most persistent are the trishaw drivers who meet passengers arriving at Kandy station. The only way to deal with touts is a very firm 'No'.

Tourists, as wealthy foreigners, can expect to attract their fair share of beggars. Remember that genuine beggars are especially pleased to receive food of any sort since they can eat it on the spot without having to share it with the racketeer who usually takes most of their earnings.

Begging rackets exist mainly in Colombo, so you might consider carrying a bag of oranges to hand to beggars instead of cash. If you are feeling charitable, you can always leave a donation in a temple or a church.

WOMEN TRAVELLERS

Generally, female travellers to Sri Lanka will be treated with great courtesy and respect. However, Sri Lankan society is conservative and the way you dress contributes greatly to

Street scene, Bandarawela

people's opinions of you, and also to the way they behave towards you. To avoid giving offence and attracting unwanted attention it is best to cover up – a good idea in the tropical sun anyway– by dressing modestly.

Female travellers in tourist spots, especially on beaches, are likely to attract stares from local men. On the West Coast, around the vicinity of Unawatuna, you may be hassled by young males.

Pests can be repelled effectively if you just walk away, avoiding contact of any sort and saying nothing. On the whole, eye contact is seen as a 'come-on', so even if simply walking along the road, avoid looking at men who are strangers.

You may find yourself the victim of opportunistic groping on a crowded bus or train. Deal with this by drawing attention to the perpetrator and his actions. Be wary of the male who sits beside you when there are plenty of seats elsewhere. Your refusal or reluctance to move away will be interpreted as an invitation to take matters further.

SHOPPING ADVICE

However exotic you think ivory chess pieces or a coral ashtray may look on the mantelpiece at home, resist the temptation to buy them, even when they are sold in top-class hotels or government shops. It is only by boycotting such products that threatened species have any chance of survival. You could regret the purchase when you arrive at the airport in Colombo, where fines of Rs 10,000 can be levied.

Under the CITES (Convention on International Trade in Endangered Species) agreement, it is forbidden to export certain animals or plants dead or alive. These include leopard skins, claws, teeth and bones as jewellery pendants, tortoise shells, leather goods made from crocodile, monitor lizard

and snakeskin, birds' feathers, elephant teeth and certain orchids. The export of live animals such as parrots, coral fish or reptiles is also banned.

For further information, contact the Wildlife and Nature Protection Society, Marine Drive, Colombo 1, tel: 01 325 248. Department of Wildlife Conservation, 493 T.B. Jaya Mawatha, Colombo 10, tel: 01 694 241, 691 321.

You will also be subject to the CITES agreement when you return home. There has been a rapid increase in plant and animal smuggling and the penalties can be severe.

Antiques may only be exported if special permission has been granted. An antique is defined as anything older than 50 years – for example, books and palm leaf manuscripts.

For information about export licences for antiques, contact the Archaeological Commissioner, Sir Marcus Fernando Mawatha, Colombo 7, tel: 694 727.

For further information on customs regulations, contact Customs House, Times of Ceylon Building, Bristol St, Colombo 1, tel: 01 421 141.

TOILETS

Toilets in up-market hotels and restaurants in tourist spots are Western-style. In less-visited areas, expect to squat Eastern-style, with water provided in place of toilet paper (so carry some with you if you prefer to use it). Public toilets are best used only in an emergency.

Travellers with disabilities

Sri Lanka is not well equipped for visitors with physical disabilities. Only a few of the five-star hotels have access and facilities for people in wheelchairs – public transport has none, so a car and driver are essential. Consult a specialist travel agent for more information.

ACCOMMODATION

Huts and grand hotels

Whether you are a backpacker or a millionaire, prefer mosquito nets or air-conditioning, the variety of accommodation is overwhelming with something to suit every purse. In Colombo and in the tourist citadels along the west and southwest coast, you will find the full spectrum – luxury 5-star hotels with executive suites, mid-range hotels offering Sri Lankan and Western-style entertainment, and the most simple type of family-run accommodation with Asian-style toilets where you have to squat.

With luck you will find yourself in reasonably priced accommodation and in an idyllic setting – cabins and palm trees or veranda rooms by the lagoon – but you may have to do without hot water. You can find a double room with bath, balcony and breakfast for about £7/US$10 in many of the smaller guesthouses, but you may need to spend some time looking.

HOTEL STANDARDS

If you are very fussy about hotel standards, then you may well be unhappy holidaying in Sri Lanka. The standards and classification categories do not always correspond with European levels. Sometimes the staff forget to clean the bath every day and towels (almost certainly freshly washed) smell unmistakably earthy. If you cannot turn a blind eye to these minor deficiencies, then a polite reference to the problem will almost certainly bring a prompt response.

It is difficult to keep undesirable room companions such as cockroaches at bay even if high cleaning standards are maintained. Always keep your bags locked and check your shoes to avoid any crawling surprises. The larger hotels have their own large generators to cope with the frequent power cuts. If you have high expectations, accommodation at below £20/US$30 per night is unlikely to be acceptable. Hardened travellers could probably find somewhere to sleep in Colombo for about £2/$3.

BOOKING TIPS

Although finding somewhere to stay in Sri Lanka does not usually present any problems, during the high season (December to January on the southwest coast, July and August in the mountains and in the 'Cultural Triangle', March to May in Nuwara Eliya), book your hotel well in advance if you have somewhere special in mind.

If you are touring outside these months, then a booking made on the preceding day should suffice. In the off-peak season haggling can probably produce a reduction of up to 30 percent.

Colonial Charm

Typical of the Sri Lankan hotel scene are the relics from the colonial era. Grand buildings, former governors' mansions, such as the Galle Face Hotel in Colombo, the Mount Lavinia south of the capital and the slightly more modest 'Resthouses'. Brass fittings on the doors, whirring ceiling fans, plush carpets, but also creaking floorboards and rusted window hinges enable guests to savour the faded charm of a past generation. They are delightful places for those who do not like the impersonal atmosphere of modern hotels.

Planning laws have spared Sri Lanka from the scourge of multi-storey hotel blocks. No hotel may exceed the height of the palm trees. The design should conform with traditional style and use as much timber as possible.

Prices have generally been increasing rapidly for some years now. The *Accommodation Guide*, published half-yearly by the Ceylon Tourist Board, provides a good, useful summary of all hotels and guesthouses in Sri Lanka.

Hotel selection

The following are suggestions for some of the most popular destinations in this guide. They are listed according to three categories: $$$ = expensive, $$ = moderate, $ = inexpensive.

Colombo

Ceylon Intercontinental, Janadhipathi Mawatha, Colombo 1, tel: 421 221, fax: 447 326. Homely hotel with good service and a pleasant lounge bar. $$$.

Colombo Hilton, Lotus Road, Colombo 1, tel: 544 644, fax: 544 657. Colombo's most glamorous hotel, with seven good restaurants, bar and nightclub. $$$.

Galadari, 64 Lotus Road, Colombo 1, tel: 544 544, fax: 498 75. Five-star luxury with a view of the sea and harbour. Exquisite Spice Market restaurant serves Sri Lankan specialities. Live music. Open weekdays noon–3pm and daily 7–11pm. $$$.

Galle Face, 2 Galle Face Centre Road, Colombo 3, tel: 541 010, fax: 541 072. Magnificent old colonial building with huge rooms beside the Indian Ocean. A charming reminder of times long gone, particularly the 'residential suites'. $$$.

Grand Oriental, 2 York Street, Colombo 1, tel: 320 391–3, fax: 447 640. Tasteful furnishings behind a classical facade, romantic candlelit dinners with a harbour view. Every Saturday evening grand Sri Lankan buffet for Rs 440. Book in advance for Harbour Room Restaurant. $$$.

Renuka, 328 Galle Road, Colombo 3, tel: 573 598–9, fax: 574 137. Good, centrally located, mid-range hotel with pleasant atmosphere (reservation recommended). $$.

Nippon, 123 Kumaran Ratnam Road, Colombo 2, tel: 431 887, fax: 332 603. Good value, central hotel in old building with flower-laden wrought iron balconies. $.

YWCA, 7 Rotunda Gardens, Colombo 3, tel: 323 498. Central accommodation. Also simple family rooms with bathroom and fan. Quiet garden with great view. $.

Sunetra & Sepala Ilangakoon, 97/1 Rosmead Place, Colombo 7, (Cinnamon Gardens), tel: 694 749, fax: 502 265. A superb hotel in modern Sri Lankan style, three large airy rooms with bath and fan. Run by a pleasant and welcoming family. $.

Kandy

The Citadel, 124 Srimath Kuduratwatte Mawatha, tel: 343 66, fax: 01 447 087. Set in the hills above the Mahaweli Ganga with traditional, tastefully furnished rooms. Quiet and exclusive. $$$.

Suisse Hotel, 30 Sangaraja Mawatha, tel: 222 637, fax: 232 083. Nice, old colonial hotel by the lake. Rooms with older, solid furniture or modern styles, large swimming pool in the garden. $$.

Queen's Hotel, Dalada Veediya, tel: 233 290, fax: 232 079. Colonial-style hotel in the heart of Kandy. $$.

Blue Heaven Guesthouse, 30/2 Poorna Lane, tel: 232 453, fax: 232 343. Twenty minutes' walk from Kandy Lake. Five small rooms with bath and splendid terrace view. $.

Regent Lodge, 172 Riverdale Road, Anniewatte, tel: 08 232 032, fax: 08 233 213. Tastefully decorated little guest house which serves wonderful meals. $.

Negombo

Royal Oceanic, Ethukala, tel: 031 79000–3, fax: 799 99. Good-value stylish hotel. Swimming pool. $$$.

Sunflower Beach, 289 Lewis Place, tel: 031 38154, 24308, fax: 38154. Rooms with balcony. Large swimming pool with sea view. $$.

Anuradhapura

Tissawewa Resthouse, Old Town, tel: 025 22299, fax: 587 613, 23265. Country house by the Tissa Wewa. Restaurant. $$.

Several small, pleasant **guesthouses** ($) along Harishandra Mawatha.

Habarana

The Lodge, Habarana, tel/fax: 025 64220. Luxurious and spacious chalets with terrace, set in parkland. Safaris, cycles, tennis court and fishing available. $$$.

The Royal Lotus, Giritale, tel: 027 46316, fax: 01 448 815. Beside Giritale Tank. Quiet and elegant. $$$.

Giritale, National Holiday Resort, Giritale, tel: 027 46311, fax: 46086. Above Giritale Tank. Simple rooms with bath, swimming pool. $$.

Polonnaruwa

Polonnaruwa Resthouse, by the tank, tel: 027 22299, fax: 01 503 504. Simple but large rooms. Sea view from the airy veranda, pleasant atmosphere. Advance booking recommended. $.

Sigiriya

Sigiriya Village, Sigiriya, tel: 066 30803, fax: 31803 and 01 683 260. An attractive complex with bungalows and swimming pool situated at the foot of Sigiriya Rock. $$$.

Nuwara Eliya

Always book in advance for rooms required between March and May and expect 100 percent price supplements.

Grand Hotel, tel: 052 22881–7, fax: 222 65. A colonial gem. Crystal chandeliers, heavy curtains, velvet easy chairs, thick pile carpet and rap music in the lobby. $$$.

Tea Factory, Kandapola,14km (9 miles) from Nuwara Eliya, tel: 052 23600, fax: 22026. The abandoned Heathersett tea factory has been converted into a modern hotel with 57 rooms. Ideal starting point for walks in the hill country. $$$.

Glendower, 5 Grand Hotel Road, tel: 052 22501, fax: 22749. A small country house with garden, fireplace and 13 very pleasant rooms, thankfully equipped with electric blankets! Early booking recommended ($$ in summer). $$$.

Cey Bank Rest, New Bazar Street, tel: 052 3053. Colonial villa with elegant mahogany furniture and parquet floors in vast rooms ($$ early summer). $.

Dickoya

Brown's Upper Glencairn Bungalow, Dickoya, Wanaraja Estate. By the road to the district hospital, tel: 0512 2348 and 01 447 845. Beautiful house in colonial style with nine rooms, restaurant, open fire and garden. Book two to three weeks in advance. $.

Bandarawela

Hotel Bandarawela, 14 Welimada Road, Bandarawela, tel: 057 22501, fax: 22834. Worth coming here if only for the brass beds. In fact, all the furniture and fittings are from a bygone age. The hotel is situated on a steep hill above the town and has a magnificent garden. $$.

Ella Resthouse, Ella, tel: 057 22636, fax: 01 503 504. Six rooms and terrace with view into the Ella Gorge. $$.

Lizzie Villa Guest House, Ella, tel: 057 23243. Peaceful accommodation and excellent food served on veranda overlooking herb garden. $.

Badulla
Duhinda Falls Inn, Bandaranaike Mawatha, Badulla, tel: 055 23028, fax: 01 22718. Some way out of town. Restaurant and bar. $.

Ratnapura
Rathnaloka Tour Inns, Kosgala-Kahangama, Ratnapura, tel/fax: 045 22455, fax: 22350. Six km (4 miles) from the town. In a delightful hilly setting. Swimming pool and restaurant. $$.

Mount Lavinia
Mount Lavinia Hotel, 102 Hotel Road, tel: 01 715 221–7, fax: 738 228. Almost 300 rooms, of which five are country-style suites with parquet floor and canopy bed. Shopping arcade and private beach. Higher rates in the modern wing of the hotel and throughout the hotel at Christmas and the New Year. $$–$$$.
Blue Seas Guest House, De Saram Road (off Beach Road), tel: 716 298. Well run and friendly guest house with 20 rooms. $.

Kalutara
Tangerine Beach Hotel, St Abew's Drive, Waskaduwa, tel: 034 22295, fax: 26794. Spacious hotel with large garden in a palm grove. Swimming pool. $$$.
Hotel Mermaid, north Kalutara, tel/fax: 034 439 792. Good mid-range hotel, where in the morning macaque monkeys hunt over the roof. Swimming pool. $$.

Bentota
Ceysands, Bentota, tel: 034 75073–4, fax: 75395 and 01 447 087. Set on a 50-m (160-ft) peninsula between the river and the Indian Ocean. Elegant rooms with columns, white tiles and balcony. Good value hotel with good restaurant. $$$.

Eden Hotel, Beruwala, tel: 76075–6, fax: 01 333 324. Pure paradise. A magnificent lobby welcomes guests to this luxury hotel, which boasts an extensive poolside area. All-round splendour. $$$.
Robinson Club Bentota, also on the peninsula, tel: 034 75167–71, fax: 75172. Extensive chalet complex in traditional Sri Lankan style. Lots of palmyra, a hatchery, plus entertainment programme. $$$.
Taj Exotica, Bentota, tel: 75650, fax: 75160. Luxurious hotel beside a great beach, with shopping centre and restaurants specialising in seafood and Chinese dishes. $$$.
Hemadan, Alutgama, opposite Ceysands on the other bank, tel/fax: 034 75320. Pleasant guesthouse in hacienda style with clean rooms and bath. Restaurant with view over the river. Own landing stage with ferry to Bentota beach. $$.
Aida Ayurveda Hotel, tel: 034 71136, fax: 034 71140. All-inclusive *ayurvedic* packages in a lovely hotel comprising linked pavilions by the river. Good restaurant. $.
Nilwala Hotel, Beruwala, tel: 034 75017, fax: 70408. Ten rooms with bath, balconies with river view. $.
Riverside Bungalows, near Ceysands, reservations can be made through P. Talans Priynandana, 90A Kaluwamodara, Alutgama. Small, quiet rooms in a garden of palm trees beside the beach. Open-air bath with mosquito net, breakfast included. Transfers to and from the airport can be arranged. $.

Ahungalla
Triton, tel: 09 64041–4, fax: 64046. Good restaurant. $$$.
Lotus Villa, tel: 09 64082, fax: 64088. Small attractive hotel complex by the beach, with swimming pool and *ayurvedic* treatment. $$.

Ambalangoda

Ambalangoda Resthouse, Main Street, tel: 09 27299. Simple hotel by the sea with rather run-down rooms, bathroom included. $.

Hikkaduwa

Lawrence Hill Paradise, 47 Waulagoda Middle Road, tel/fax: 074 383 299. Small but attractive hotel in an exotic garden set back from the coast, with 20 rooms and swimming pool. $$$.

Reefcomber, Galle Road, tel: 09 77377–8, tel/fax: 09 77374. Unusual rooms. Large swimming pool by the sea ($$$ in winter). $$.

Blue Corals, 332 Galle Road, tel: 09 77679, 01 648 301, fax: 01 647 972. Nice rooms. View over the coral banks from the balcony. Small swimming pool in the garden ($$$ in winter). $$.

Moon Beam, 458/1 Galle Road, Hikkaduwa-Narigama, tel: 078 76938. Five very clean and tastefully furnished rooms with tiled bathroom. Small garden by the beach. $$.

Galle

Closenberg Hotel, Matara Road, Magalle, climb the steep drive on the left near the harbour entrance, tel/fax: 09 32241. An 1850s villa with garden. Old rooms on the ground floor, modern rooms above with balcony and bay view. $$.

New Oriental Hotel, 10 Church Street, Fort, tel/fax: 09 22059. Victorian splendour, plus attractive garden and swimming pool. $$.

Unawatuna

Unawatuna Beach Resort, Parangiyawatte, tel: 09 24028, tel/fax: 09 32247. Spacious and tasteful rooms, some with sea view. $$.

Sun'n'Sea, tel: 09 53200, fax: 53399. Magnificent spot at the eastern end of the bay. A change from the dull, uni-fied style seen in Unawatuna. Country-style furnishings, large rooms with bathroom, pleasant terrace and rattan rocking chairs. Good veranda restaurant with bay view. $.

Ahangama

Hotel Club Lanka, Ahangama, tel: 09 53296, fax: 53361. By the beach. Large pool. Breakfast included. $$.

Tangalla

Palm Paradise Cabanas, just before Tangalla, tel/fax: 047 40338. Attractive octagonal timber bungalows on stilts. Idyllic location in a shady palm grove by the beach. Breakfast and dinner included. $$.

Tangalla Bay Hotel, Tangalla, tel/fax: 047 40346. Unusual, 1970s-style hotel. On a cliff at the end of the bay. Restaurant and small pool. Simple rooms with terrace. $$.

Some small guesthouses nearby.

Tissamaharama/Tissa Wewa

Resthouse, by the shores of Tissa Wewa, tel: 047 37299, fax: 01 422 732. Modern, popular hotel with swimming pool and lake view. Booking in advance recommended. $$.

Taprobane Guesthouse, opposite the Resthouse. Clean, simple rooms with bath, fan and mosquito net. Breakfast included. Very helpful staff. $.

Yala National Park

Yala Safari Beach Hotel, Yala, tel/fax: 047 20471, fax: 01 345729. Near the entrance to Yala National Park, ground-level rooms with small veranda. Many coach parties, so book well in advance. $$$.

Nilaveli

Nilaveli Beach Hotel, Nilaveli, tel: 026 22071, fax: 026 32297, 01 448 279. Almost 100 rooms, two of which are luxury suites. Swimming pool. $$.

✵ INSIGHT COMPACT GUIDES

Great Little Guides to the following destinations:

Algarve	Goa	St Petersburg	North York Moors
Amsterdam	Gran Canaria	Salzburg	Northumbria
Athens	Greece	Shanghai	Oxford
Bahamas	Holland	Singapore	Peak District
Bali	Hong Kong	Southern Spain	Scotland
Bangkok	Ibiza	Sri Lanka	Scottish
Barbados	Iceland	Switzerland	Highlands
Barcelona	Ireland	Sydney	Shakespeare
Beijing	Israel	Tenerife	Country
Belgium	Italian Lakes	Thailand	Snowdonia
Berlin	Italian Riviera	Toronto	South Downs
Bermuda	Jamaica	Turkey	York
Brittany	Jerusalem	Turkish Coast	Yorkshire Dales
Bruges	Kenya	Tuscany	
Brussels	Laos	Venice	_USA regional_
Budapest	Lisbon	Vienna	_titles:_
Burgundy	Madeira	Vietnam	Boston
California	Madrid	West of Ireland	Cape Cod
Cambodia	Mallorca		Chicago
Chile	Malta	_UK regional_	Florida
Copenhagen	Menorca	_titles:_	Florida Keys
Costa Brava	Milan	Bath &	Hawaii – Maui
Costa del Sol	Montreal	Surroundings	Hawaii – Oahu
Costa Rica	Morocco	Belfast	Las Vegas
Crete	Moscow	Cambridge &	Los Angeles
Cuba	Munich	East Anglia	Martha's Vineyard
Cyprus	Normandy	Cornwall	& Nantucket
Czech Republic	Norway	Cotswolds	Miami
Denmark	Paris	Devon & Exmoor	New Orleans
Dominican	Poland	Edinburgh	New York
Republic	Portugal	Glasgow	San Diego
Dublin	Prague	Guernsey	San Francisco
Egypt	Provence	Jersey	Washington DC
Finland	Rhodes	Lake District	
Florence	Rio de Janeiro	London	
French Riviera	Rome	New Forest	

Insight's checklist to meet all your travel needs:

■ _Insight Guides_ provide the complete picture, with expert cultural background and stunning photography. Great for travel planning, for use on the spot, and as a souvenir. 180 titles.

■ _Insight Pocket Guides_ focus on the best choices for places to see and things to do, picked by our correspondents. They include large fold-out maps. More than 120 titles.

■ _Insight Compact Guides_ are fact-packed books to carry with you for easy reference when you're on the move in a destination. More than 130 titles.

■ _Insight Maps_ combine clear, detailed cartography with essential information and a laminated finish that makes the maps durable and easy to fold. 125 titles.

■ _Insight Phrasebooks_ and _Insight Travel Dictionaries_ are very portable and help you find exactly the right word in French, German, Italian and Spanish.

The world's largest collection of visual travel guides and maps

INDEX